federally administered tribal areas

(FATA)

LOCAL REGION HANDBOOK / A Guide to the People and the Agencies

Federally Administered Tribal Areas

Kapisa

Kunar

Laghman

Khar — **Bajaur**

North West Frontier Province

Kabul

Nangarhar

Ghalani ● **Mohmand**

Logar

Khyber

Landi Kotal

FR Peshawar

Paktia

● Parachinar

● Kalaya

FR Kohat

Khost

Orakzai

FR Bannu

Kurram

Paktika

Miranshah ●

FR Lakki Marwat

North Waziristan

South Waziristan

FR Tank

Wana ●

FR Dera Ismail Khan

Baluchistan

Punjab

Federally Administered Tribal Areas

——	Roads
	Agency Borders
- - -	Frontier Region (FR) Borders
——	River
┼┼┼	Railroad
●	Agency Headquarters
	Frontier Region (FR)
	Afghanistan
) (	Khyber Pass
	Agency or Frontier Region (FR) Name

Table of Contents

List of Tables and Maps

LIST OF TABLES

LIST OF MAPS

Cover and Title Page Photographs by Anthony Maw

Guide to the Handbook

This handbook is a concise field guide to the Federally Administered Tribal Areas (FATA) of Pakistan. Along with our companion handbook on the North West Frontier Province (NWFP), this handbook is intended to help orient and inform civilian and military personnel who are engaged in the Afghanistan-Pakistan region (AfPak).

Setting policy and managing field operations in Afghanistan and Pakistan requires understanding the human dynamics in the Pashtun border areas. FATA/NWFP is the hub for Taliban insurgent activity in both countries. Understanding the history, people, politics and economics of FATA/NWFP and why it is a base for militant extremists, will inform a counterinsurgency strategy in the border area and inform efforts to overcome militant influence across the region.

Civilians and military in Afghanistan will better recognize how the security, political and economic networks in FATA and NWFP influence and relate to the situation in the border provinces of Afghanistan. Readers will better appreciate and consider the strategic effects of operations on both sides of the border. When engaging Pashtun leaders in Afghanistan, readers will better recognize the nature and importance of interests and influence extending across the border to FATA and NWFP.

Policy makers and program managers engaged with Pakistan will better understand how the political, cultural and economic dimensions of FATA/NWFP foster its militant character. As in any counterinsurgency campaign, separating the people from the insurgency depends as much on the political and economic activities as security operations. The handbook will help readers understand who and what matters within FATA/NWFP, political and economic conditions and issues that shape the environment in FATA/NWFP, and the how and why of influencing militancy in the border areas.

SOURCES AND DATA

Key sources for this guide include Islamic Republic of Pakistan Government, non-government organizations (NGOs), academic and United States government (USG) publications. The book reflects information and perspectives from Pakistani and international experts who have spent significant time on the ground in and around FATA.

The authors and editors of this handbook aim to present accurate and credible information. The region is in transition and difficult to access, so there are varying viewpoints about the "ground truth" in FATA and adjoining areas. We present government data to inform and orient, but we do not endorse its accuracy. Different groups – religious, insurgent, militant, political and governmental – are trying to secure and expand their influence in FATA, and scenarios in various parts of FATA are changing quickly. The handbook focuses on providing basic information and a knowledge base that can be built upon, using, among other things, the list of recommended references and internet sites listed in the Appendix.

Information in this book is unclassified. The views and opinions expressed in this booklet are those of the authors and in no way reflect the views of the United States government.

THE ELECTRONIC UPDATE

Look for electronic updates to this book at *www.idsinternational.net/ afpakbooks*. Updates will cover any new developments, issues, and leaders that have emerged after publication. They will also provide corrections and expanded content in key areas based on feedback from readers.

We hope the handbook will continue to be a valuable tool in thinking about the challenges in FATA. If you have questions, comments or feedback for future updates or editions please email *afpakbooks@ idsinternational.net*.

ABOUT IDS INTERNATIONAL

Publisher of Afghanistan Provincial Handbook Series and the FATA/NWFP Pakistan Books

This book is part of a series of handbooks on Afghanistan and Pakistan provinces and regions. Afghanistan province titles include Ghazni, Helmand, Kandahar, Khost, Kunar, Laghman, Nangarhar, Nuristan, Paktika, and Paktya.

In addition to publishing these handbooks, IDS International provides training and support to government agencies in the areas of politics, economics, culture, stability operations, reconstruction, counterinsurgency and interagency relations. In particular, IDS is a leading trainer of the US military in working with Provincial Reconstruction Teams (PRTs) in Iraq and Afghanistan. IDS offers its clients expertise and experience in non-lethal dimensions of counterinsurgency and interagency collaboration in complex operations. The writers and editors on this project offer a lifetime of experience working in these provinces and share a dedication to bringing peace and prosperity to the people of Afghanistan and Pakistan.

Author: Hasan Faqeer
Editors: Nick Dowling and Amy Frumin
Editorial Reviews: Imtiaz Ali, Peter Bergen, and Bob Grenier
Assistant Editors: Tom Viehe and Katie Stout

IDS INTERNATIONAL GOVERNMENT SERVICES
1916 Wilson Boulevard
Suite 302
Arlington, VA 22201
703-875-2212
www.idsinternational.net
afpakbooks@idsinternational.net

PUBLISHED: JUNE 2009

This and other AfPak handbooks may be bought in either digital or hard copy format. Samples are available upon request. IDS International provides analysis to government and private organizations in the areas of politics, economics, culture, stability operations, reconstruction, counterinsurgency and interagency relations. For inquiries, please email *afpakbooks@idsinternational.net* or call 703-875-2212.

The Khyber Gate sits at the mouth of the Khyber Pass in Jamrud. The most vital link between Afghanistan and Pakistan, the Khyber Pass has historically served as a corridor for both invasion and commerce.

PHOTO BY ANTHONY MAW

Chapter 1
Orientation and Overview

The Federally Administered Tribal Areas (FATA) of Pakistan are a strategically important sliver of land separating Pakistan's North West Frontier Province (NWFP) from eastern Afghanistan. The terrain of FATA is picturesque. Rivers cut into mountains, forming small basins and valleys checkered with settlements and farmland. It is home to about five million Pashtun tribesmen and thousands of Afghan refugees.

FATA holds strategic importance because of the Pashtun tribes straddling the border between Pakistan and Afghanistan. The Pashtuns are conservative Muslims with a long tradition of defending their mountains from invaders. Today, FATA is the base for Taliban insurgencies in both countries and a sanctuary for al-Qaeda. The contemporary influence of militant Islam in this region dates to when FATA launched, supported and provided sanctuary to the mujahedin resistance to the 1979 Soviet invasion of Afghanistan.

Although largely under Taliban and tribal influence, FATA is officially managed and controlled by the president of Pakistan through the governor of NWFP. FATA is divided into seven agencies (districts): Bajaur, Mohmand, Khyber, Orakzai, Kurram, North Waziristan, and South Waziristan. All but Orakzai agency share a border with Afghanistan, and each has a dominant tribe or tribal group, economic base, and physical characteristics that distinguish it from the others. FATA shares a border with five Afghan provinces to its north and west: Kunar, Nangarhar, Paktya, Khost, and Paktika. Both sides of the border are inhabited predominantly by Pashtuns.

Harsh geography, poor infrastructure, lack of public investment, perennial tribal disputes, and regional conflicts all combine to drive a wedge between FATA and the rest of Pakistan. These factors have led to the sense of deprivation among the local people in FATA. They feel discriminated against and, as a consequence, disconnected from the rest of the country. Today, FATA is among Pakistan's most under-developed areas. Its peculiar, semi-autonomous constitutional status and its colonial-era legal system further isolate it from the rest of Pakistan. FATA's isolation and lack of development may correlate with the appeal of extremism in this region.

Sympathy for Pashtuns in Afghanistan across the Durand Line (AfPak border) is strong. The pro-Pashtun orientation often manifests as an anti-US/NATO sentiment and an anti-Pakistani government senti-ment. Consequently, government legitimacy continues to diminish in FATA and pro-government elements are regularly targeted and killed. Ordinary residents of FATA consider themselves caught in the middle of a battle between Taliban/al-Qaeda elements and Pakistan's security forces. Similarly, the US/NATO presence in Afghanistan and controversial drone attacks in FATA are seen in terms of direct military confrontation with the US. Security from Taliban intimidation is a critical concern.

ORIENTATION

The geography of FATA channels human interaction into three zones: northern, central, and southern. Most parts of FATA are arid and semi-arid, with warm summers and cool winters, although areas in the central zone can be humid at times. The people in each of these three zones are more integrated and connected with each other than with people of other zones of FATA or Pakistan. The people from the northern zone are particularly isolated. A road system does not connect the seven tribal agencies. The roads are in poor condition, and people from FATA prefer to travel via NWFP before entering another agency from a nearby point in the province. In the 2008-09 budget, 177 road plans in FATA were financially sanctioned by the national government to make the area more accessible and to link its villages, towns, and commercial centers with each other. Work on most of these projects has not started yet due to conflict and resistance from FATA tribesmen, who believe these roads will help the army move its convoys.

In the northern zone of Bajaur and Mohmand agencies, foothills form a transition zone between the majestic Hindu Kush mountains and the lowland basins. The Panjkora River winds through these mountains with run-off from the Hindu Kush, gathering in the Jandool River and its tributaries. The Kabul River enters Pakistan just north of the Khyber Pass, gathering local rivers like the Bara River and seasonal streams. This zone borders the Afghan provinces of Kunar and Nangarhar. No border crossings like Khyber Pass exist in this zone.

Khyber, Kurram, and Orakzai agencies make up the central zone. The Safed Koh mountains stretch eastward from Afghanistan, running parallel to the Kabul River. The Bara, Khanki, Kurram, and Mastura river valleys provide their residents with the most extensively culti-vated land in FATA. This zone borders Paktya and Khost provinces in Afghanistan.

North and South Waziristan make up the southern zone of the FATA. The barren, high Waziristan hills form rugged gorges, creating a geographic body unto themselves, separate from the Safed Koh of the north and Sulaiman Range of the south. The Gomal and Tochi Rivers pass through these hills and connect Waziristan to Khost and Paktika.

TRIBAL AGENCIES

According to the 1998 census, the total population of the FATA is 3,176,331. It was estimated by the Pakistani government in 2000 to be about 3,341,070 people, but independent sources from the area estimate the actual figure to be roughly five million, or three percent of Pakistan's population. It is the most rural administrative unit in Pakistan; only 3.1 percent of the population reside in established townships.

Bajaur Agency

Smallest of all of the FATA agencies in size (1,290 sq. km.), Bajaur is largely inaccessible due to its mountainous terrain and extreme weather. Bajaur is home to three main tribes: Tarkani in the north, Uthmankhel in the southeast, and Mamund in the southwest. It has a mostly rural population that grow wheat and maize. Many people also grow opium when possible. Many Bajauris leave the agency to find employment, usually in Peshawar and Karachi. Bajaur's administrative headquarters is in Khar, a town 140 km north of Peshawar. Traffic to and from neighboring Kunar province in Afghanistan frequently runs through the unpaved Nawa Pass. Major towns (with markets and a population of over 10,000 people) of Bajaur include Khar, Raghagan, Hajilawant, and Jar. Of these, Khar is the most developed and important town of Bajaur.

Table 1. Agencies of FATA

AGENCY/FR	CAPITAL	AREA (SQ KM)	POPULATION (1998 EST)	POPULATION DENSITY (PER SQ KM)	ANNUAL GROWTH RATE, 1981–98
Bajaur	Khar	1,290	595,227	461	4.33%
Khyber	Landi Kotal	2,576	546,730	212	3.92%
Kurram	Parachinar	3,380	448,310	133	2.50%
Mohmand	Ghalanai	2,296	334,453	146	4.28%
North Waziristan	Miranshah	4,707	361,246	77	2.46%
Orakzai	Kohat-Thall road	1,538	225,441	147	- 2.69%
South Waziristan	Wana and Tank	6,620	429,841	65	1.95%
Total		**22,407**	**2,941,248**	**117**	**2.19%**

Mohmand Agency

Known for its rugged mountains and barren slopes, Mohmand is home to many passes, historically providing routes to and from Central Asia for warriors, traders, and merchants. Home to the Mohmand tribe, Mohmand is divided into Lower and Upper Mohmand. Lower Mohmand has fertile land, fed by the Kabul River on the agency's southern border. Upper Mohmand is rocky and less productive due to the scarcity of water. Due to lack of rainfall in recent years, many have been left jobless, and some have migrated to Shabqadar and Peshawar in the NWFP.

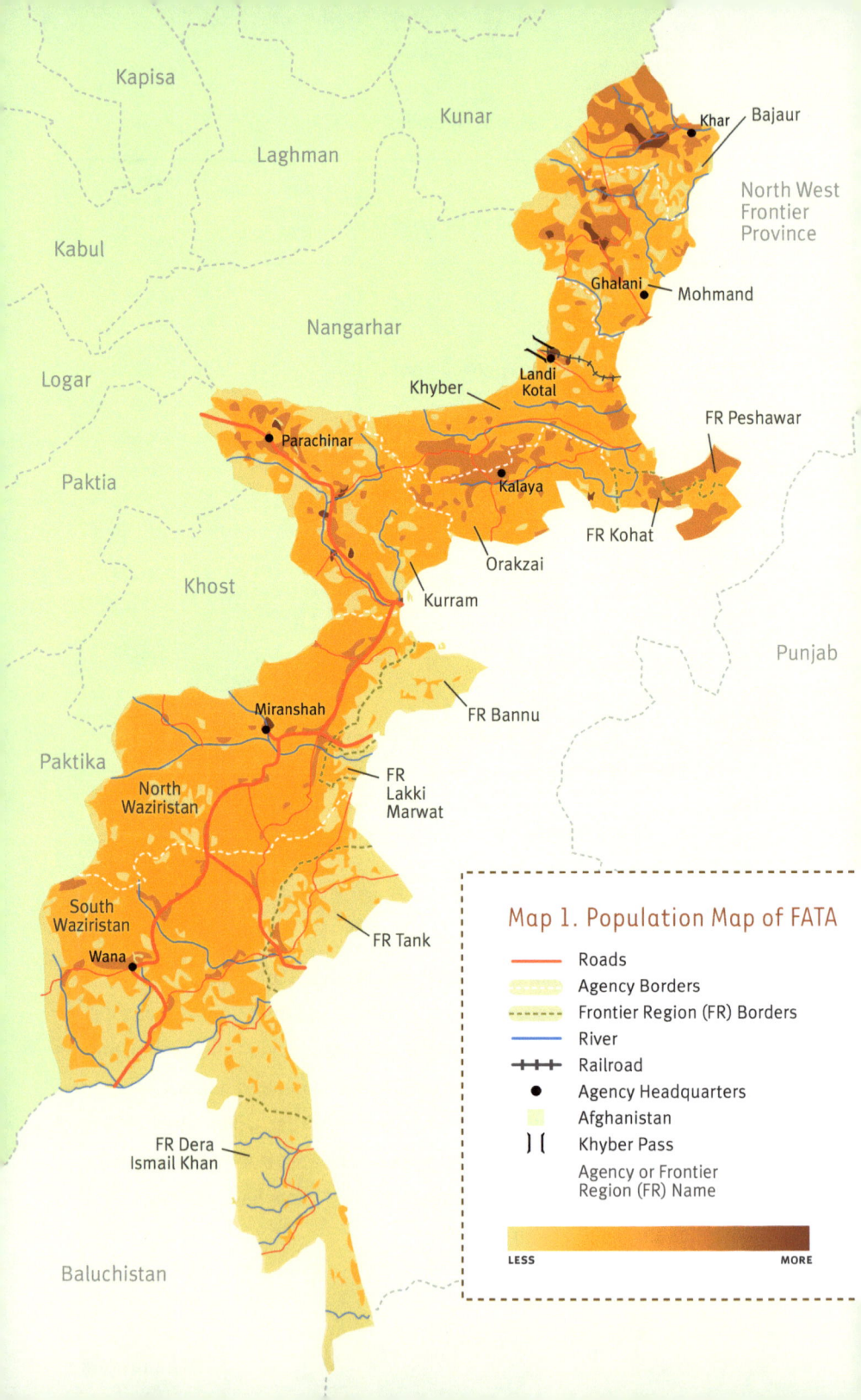

Map 1. Population Map of FATA

Roads	(red line)
Agency Borders	
Frontier Region (FR) Borders	
River	(blue line)
Railroad	
●	Agency Headquarters
	Afghanistan
) (	Khyber Pass
	Agency or Frontier Region (FR) Name

LESS — MORE

Labels on map:

Kapisa
Kunar
Laghman
North West Frontier Province
Kabul
Nangarhar
Khar — Bajaur
Ghalani — Mohmand
Logar
Khyber
Landi Kotal
FR Peshawar
Paktia
Parachinar
Kalaya
FR Kohat
Khost
Orakzai
Kurram
Punjab
FR Bannu
Miranshah
FR Lakki Marwat
Paktika
North Waziristan
FR Tank
South Waziristan
Wana
FR Dera Ismail Khan
Baluchistan

Mohmand agency shares a border with the Bajaur agency to the north, the Dir district of NWFP to the east, Peshawar district in the southeast, and Nangarhar in Afghanistan to the west. Mohmand's administrative headquarters is located in the town of Ghalanai.

Khyber Agency

Lying at the base of the Safed Koh (White Mountains or Spinghar), the Khyber agency is a hilly expanse with several fertile valleys and plains. The hills are covered with thick alpine forests, while the valleys are irrigated by the Bara and Chora Rivers and their tributaries. This area is often called the Tirah, homeland of the Afridi tribe. The Kabul River makes up the agency's northern border with Mohmand agency.

On its western border with Afghanistan is Khyber's namesake: the Khyber Pass. Leading into modern-day Nangarhar province, the Khyber Pass provides the most vital link between Afghanistan and Pakistan, historically serving as a corridor for both invasion and commerce. Alexander the Great, Genghis Khan, Tamerlane, and Mahmud Ghaznawi all used this route for entering the region. The Khyber railroad, built at an enormous cost by the British in 1920, threads its way through 34 tunnels crossing 92 bridges and culverts. The British used the railway to move troops and supplies in emergencies. Most of the people in this agency are involved in transport, smuggling, and farming. Key towns in Khyber agency include Bara, Jamrud, and Landi Kotal. Shagai Fort and Torkham, border points with Afghanistan, are also considered important areas of the agency.

Orakzai Agency

Dominated by the Karagh Ghar mountains, Orakzai agency has two main river valleys, Khanki and Mastura, with parallel ranges that are densely covered with low brushwood and groves of pines. The weather is cold in the winter, with mild rains year round.

The people in this agency are mostly farmers. The Orakzai tribesmen are known for their two-story houses made of stones and mud. The first floor is devoted to cattle and the storage of grain, while the top floor is a residence. Often built on commanding positions with well-placed towers for their protection, houses also feature *morchas* (bunkers) for defensive purposes, but are not generally walled, unlike homes throughout most of the tribal agencies. Important towns of the agency are Ghiljo, Daboori, Kalaya, Mishti Mela, and Kurez. The administrative headquarters of the agency is in Hangu district.

Kurram Agency

The Kurram River is the lifeblood of the agency and runs southeast from Kharlachi to the southeast corner near Thall. Richly irrigated, Kurram is known for its agriculture. For example, Parachinar, Kurram's administrative headquarters, is known for its apples. Bounded by the Safed Koh in the north-northeast, Kurram is divided into two parts: Upper Kurram and Lower Kurram. Upper Kurram's valley extends from Peiwar Kotal to Sadda, where Karmana River joins the Kurram River. The southern part of Upper Kurram is enclosed by high mountains on all sides. However, as you move north, the valley opens up into a sloping plain: the Parachinar Plateau. Lower Kurram extends from Sadda to Thall in Hangu district. It is narrow and hedged by low hills on either side of the Kurram River.

Kurram currently enjoys closer relations with its bordering Afghan provinces than with its Pakistani neighbors due to its discontented Shia community. In Pakistan, it borders Orakzai and Khyber agencies to the east, Hangu district to the southeast, and North Waziristan agency to the south. Important cities of the agency are Parachinar, Sadda, Alizai, Bagzai, and Dogar.

North Waziristan Agency

The second largest agency in size, it is home to high and difficult hills with deep and rugged gorges known as the Waziristan hills. The Tochi

River bisects the agency, forming the Tochi Pass, through which armies, merchants, and cultures have moved from Paktika in Afghanistan to Bannu in Pakistan. The Tochi Valley is very fertile and irrigated. The city of Razmak in the south is known as a source for many minerals. North Waziristan's administrative headquarters are at Miranshah. Due to the rugged terrain and lack of opportunity in this agency, many people go abroad to earn their livelihood.

South Waziristan Agency

Like its northern neighbor, South Waziristan has harsh and mountainous terrain, with settlements scattered across the landscape. The land rises gradually from southeast to northwest. The Preghal Range dominates along the western border with Afghanistan, while the Gomal River forms its southern boundary.

The largest agency in all of the FATA, South Waziristan has two headquarters. In the summer, the headquarters is located at Wana. In the winter, it moves to Tank due to the harsh conditions. South Waziristan borders Paktika province in Afghanistan to the west, Pakistan's Baluchistan province to the south, Dera Ismail Khan district (NWFP) to the east, and North Waziristan to the north. The people of the agency have strong ties to Afghanistan, North Waziristan, and Frontier Region Dera Ismail Khan. They have blood relatives and landed property on both sides of the Durand Line. Important cities include: Wana, Ladha, Makin, Sararogha, Azam Warsak, and Angoor Adda.

The majority of Wazirs and Mehsuds of South Waziristan are pastoral. The agency also produces or trades charcoal, wool, potatoes, chilghozas, and a few varieties of locally grown fruit. The Wazirs also breed horses and rear sheep. A large number of Mehsuds are employed in the army, as levies and *Khassadars* in local militias and as scouts in the Frontier Corps.

A border crossing on the Durand Line. The Durand Line is the dividing border between Afghanistan and Pakistan. It cuts through Pashtun tribes and families, who view it with contempt. To this day, around 10,000 Pashtuns cross the border daily.

PHOTO BY BILL SPENCE

Chapter 2
Relevant History

FROM ANCIENT TO MODERN TIMES

Pashtun warriors have traditionally resisted outsiders who use the Khyber Pass and adjoining areas to enter the Indian sub-continent. These invaders included warriors, proselytizers, and even Sufi mystics from Central Asia, Turkey, Iran, and Afghanistan. The Pashtun gateway into this part of South Asia is and has been accessible to all. However, no outsider has either settled in the area or controlled it effectively for long.

The British annexed this areas in 1848 and sought to insulate their empire's "settled areas" from both Russian expansion in Afghanistan and recurrent tribal raids. In the 1870s, the British Raj attempted to control the annexed tribal regions through the Frontier Crimes Regulations (FCR), which gave local tribal chiefs considerable power to govern so long as they met the needs of the British. The FCR prescribed special procedures for the tribal areas, distinct from the criminal and civil laws that were in force elsewhere in British India. These regulations developed the idea of collective territorial responsibility (including collective punishment) that called for dispute resolution to take place through the traditional *jirga* (council of elders). The British attained a measure of stability in the area for a period, but their rule never went unchallenged. Pashtun history celebrates the trouble they gave the British.

FATA was formally created in 1893 with the signing of the Afghanistan-UK treaty, which created the Durand Line, the border between Afghanistan and modern-day Pakistan. The Durand Line has been viewed with contempt by FATA's Pashtuns, particularly because it often divides families. Predictably, this line is a major source of a tension between Pakistan and Afghanistan. Many Afghans do not accept the Durand Line as an international border, but claim FATA and even NWFP as parts of Afghanistan. However, in 1947 (when British India was divided into Pakistan and India), FATA's tribesmen acceded to Pakistan through a jirga decision – but not before receiving certain concessions about their status within Pakistan. The NWFP was created in 1901 as a separate administrative unit. The annexed areas continued under the same FCR governance after the creation of Pakistan in 1947.

By continuing the FCR in letter and spirit, FATA received little support and payed no taxes to Pakistan. Pakistan always shied away from investing in infrastructure in the area because of scarce economic resources. FATA tribesmen, on the other hand, responded positively whenever their assistance was needed by the Pakistani government. For instance, in 1948, bands of FATA tribesmen offered their services in the disputed Kashmir region, where Pakistan and India were vying for control. On other occasions, some tribes of FATA remained difficult to handle, and in the early 1960s, the Pakistan Air Force bombed an area in modern-day Bajaur agency.

From the beginning this region remained critical for Pakistan's strategic interests with consequences for Pakistan-Afghanistan relations. Both Pakistan and Afghanistan have supported Pashtun nationalists in the tribal areas as a way to gain influence in the neighboring state.

SOVIET-AFGHAN WAR PERIOD (1979-1989)

After the 1979 Soviet invasion of Afghanistan, Muslim radicals came to Pakistan to launch a counter movement, with FATA acting as the base camp, where the geography provided cover for training camps for the fighters (known as mujahedin). Pakistan's military and intelligence agencies spearheaded this effort on the ground, with the US, Saudi Arabia, and some European and Gulf countries providing weapons and/or financial support. Within Pakistan, the conflict was sold as a war of survival necessary to prevent the spread of communism. In the process, Pakistan channeled funds and weapons to many Afghan groups of its own choice.

A *madrassa* (seminary) network also developed quickly to cater to the education and religious needs of about three million Afghan refugees that poured into FATA and NWFP between 1979 and 1989. The madrassas helped spread the Wahhabist version of Islam and generally promoted the growth of religious conservatism. Although a similar, native Deobandist strain of Islam long had a significant influence in this area, the madrassa and Wahhabi influence made an impact on the society and culture of FATA as religious zeal gained currency – especially for the purpose of inspiring young fighters.

TALIBAN RULE IN AFGHANISTAN (1994-2001)

After the Soviet withdrawal, the networks in the region strengthened further as many madrassa students (called Taliban) moved from FATA and NWFP to Afghanistan to take part in the civil war. The political rise of the Taliban in 1994-95, with official Pakistani support, also empowered FATA tribesmen who had played a role in the Afghan Jihad. Thousands of Arab and Central Asian fighters who had moved to FATA in the 1980s travelled between Kabul, Kandahar, and Jalalabad in

Afghanistan and FATA. Pakistan's interest in Afghanistan's civil war was strategic, favoring a fundamentalist Pashtun Taliban government in Kabul as a useful ally against India.

CONTEMPORARY DEVELOPMENTS

Shortly after 9/11, President Pervez Musharraf changed Pakistan's pro-Taliban policy and provided a support base for the US-led war in Afghanistan. He also unleashed his security elements against the al-Qaeda presence in the settled areas of Pakistan. However, it was difficult to extend this policy to actively work against the Taliban, given that Taliban were seen as sympathetic to Pakistan and also anti-India in their orientation. Hence parts of the army and Inter-Services Intelligence Directorate (ISI) – and perhaps even elements of the Musharraf leadership – continued tacitly supporting the Afghan Taliban behind the scenes. The most well known case is that of Jalaluddin Haqqani, a pro-Taliban Afghan militant whose close relationship with the ISI dates back to the anti-Soviet Jihad.

After the US and allied forces' military campaign in Afghanistan, Taliban leaders and foreign fighters fled to FATA, where local tribesmen readily offered them sanctuary as called for by *pashtun-wali* traditions of hospitality. The Pakistani military could neither halt the inflow of Arabs nor curb the outflow of Pashtuns who felt duty-bound to go to Kabul to rescue their brethren during the US-led campaign.

Under US pressure, Musharraf moved a larger segment of troops to FATA in 2003 and 2004 to counter the influx of foreign fighters, particularly in South Waziristan, but failed to subdue the tribes. Having defeated the Pakistani army, the newly empowered groups started altering the traditional power balance – shifting authority and control from tribal elders (a hereditary system) to young radicals. Behind religious slogans, class battles were also at play. The *maliks* are responsible for distributing financial support to those who remain loyal to the status quo and the policies of the government of Pakistan. For the past several years, there have been demands for drastic reforms in the tribal structure against the corrupt and monopolistic malik system. When the Taliban rose against the malik system and the monopoly of tribal chiefs, they were supported by an overwhelming majority in the tribal region.

The Pakistani government did not take aggressive military action against Pakistani Taliban elements in FATA because it considered them to be a strategic asset, especially against the Indian influence in Afghanistan. Likewise, the Pakistani government feared the consequences of antagonizing these militant elements while they were occupied primarily in cross-border attacks into Afghanistan. The 2009 military operation against the Taliban in Swat and FATA is Pakistan's first serious, sustained action, as the terrorist designs of native Taliban elements endangered its own stability.

Three Pashtun boys in Landi Kotal. While there are many tribes, sub-tribes and clans of Pashtuns living in FATA, all follow an ancient and chivalrous code of honor known as pashtunwali. Seen as collective wisdom from their forefathers, this code is the basis for the Pashtuns' famous hospitality and blood feuds.

PHOTO BY BILL SPENCE

Chapter 3
Ethnicity, Tribes, Languages
and Religion

FATA lies squarely in the middle of the Pashtun belt, which extends from southern Afghanistan to northern Pakistan. The roughly five million Pashtuns in FATA are divided into major and minor tribes, many of which straddle the border with Afghanistan. The Pashtuns of FATA are more conservative and tribal in character than other areas due to their relative isolation. This accentuates the role of *pashtun-wali*, the traditional Pashtun code of honor.

A total of roughly 40 million Pashtuns live in Pakistan and Afghanistan, with Pakistani Pashtuns spread across FATA, NWFP, Baluchistan, and in Karachi (Sindh province). Divided into four major branches called Sarbani, Batani, Ghorghashti, and Karlani, Pashtuns are further divided into roughly 60 major tribes and over 300 sub-tribes or clans. About 13 tribes and sub-tribes live on both sides of the Pakistan-Afghanistan border and move across the border freely. Their movement used to be regulated only through border passes called *rahdaries* (temporary travel document).

Table 2. Tribes of FATA

AGENCY/FR	TRIBES
Bajaur	Uthmankhel, Tarkani, Mamund
Mohmand	Mohmand, Safi, Uthmankhel
Khyber	Afridis, Shinwaris, Mulagooris, and Shalmanis
Orakzai	Orakzai and Bangash
Kurram	Turi, Bangash, Parachinari, and Masozai
North Waziristan	Uthmanzai Wazir, Dawar, Saidgai, Kharasin, and Gulbaz
South Waziristan	Mehsud and Ahmadzai Waziris

LANGUAGE

The term "Pashtun" refers to all tribes that speak the Pasto language, irrespective of their origin. The people of FATA largely speak Pashto, and the language is inextricably linked with the ethos and character of the people. It is also called *jaba* (literally meaning language), perceived as synonymous with the Pashtun code. To Pashtuns, *jaba* is also a word of honor – for instance, referring to someone as "not having Pashto" means somebody has no values. Broadly speaking, adherence to pashtunwali and related concepts are also intricately linked to the Pashtun identity and Pashto language.

PASHTUNWALI

Pashtunwali is an an ancient and chivalrous code of honor associated with Pashtuns. It is a social, cultural, and quasi-legal code guiding, governing, and shaping both individual and communal conduct. For Pashtuns, this is the collective wisdom of their forefathers compiled over a period of centuries. It has varied sources – ranging from Sufi poetry, folklore of epic romances, and various *mataloona* (proverbs). The major components of pashtunwali are:

Melmastia (Hospitality): Showing hospitality and profound respect to all guests, regardless of race, religion, national affiliation, or economic status, and doing so without any hope of remuneration or favor. Historically, even enemies were provided this privilege if they came to one's house.

Badal (Revenge): Avenging a wrong is an individual obligation. This requirement has no time limits. There are many known cases in FATA where families took revenge after decades, and minor differences or perceived insults turned into blood feuds that engulfed whole tribes.

Nanawatay (Sanctuary): Protection is given to a person who requests it against one's enemies. Any visitor to the area in a difficult situation can ask for sanctuary after telling locals that the person meant no harm to the people of the area. That person is protected at all costs and under any circumstances. Arab and Central Asian fighters are under this protection in parts of FATA – especially in the Waziristan agencies. In some cases, Pashtuns have offered this privilege to Western security and NGO workers.

Zemaka (Land/Earth): Defend land and property from incursions.

Nang (Honor): Safeguard the honor of the family – in terms of independence, culture and religion. This can be interpreted widely or narrowly depending upon the education and exposure of a person.

Additional Codes

Torah (Courage): Tradition of bravery and courage in the face of challenge.

Hujra (a sitting place or community hall): A meeting place or assembly hall where any member of the community can come and discuss cultural or political issues. It also acts as a forum for conflict resolution and negotiation. The host of the *hujra* has specific responsibilities, especially regarding the safety of all visitors.

Various additional qualifications of pashtunwali are: *saree-tob* (manhood, chivalry); *khpelwaki* (self authority); *jirga* (decision-making through an assembly of elders); *roogha* (need for reconciliation or compromise); *barabari* (equivalence); *ghairat* (pride); *gwanditob* (regard for neighbors); *oogha warkawel* (giving a lift to people in need); *ashar* (collective, co-operative work); *zhamena* (commitment).

Among these many features, the strongest are a refusal to accept outside interference in internal matters, disdain and reluctance to be governed by a distant central authority, and an amazing confidence in the ability of local leaders to provide protection and an environment in which people can live according to their own traditions and practices. To this pre-Islamic code, they have added some aspects of the Islamic law, *sharia*. According to critics, the only religious notions picked up were those that work well with pashtunwali code.

The tribes in FATA are organized through their *maliks*, who are either selected by the tribes themselves or, on some occasions, appointed by government representatives (political agents) as a favor. This leadership group is increasingly losing its hold on tribes because religious leaders are gaining recognition and loyalty. Nevertheless, the system of tribal hierarchy and organization is expected to remain relevant for the foreseeable future.

TRIBES

The **Tarkani** are an offshoot of the Yousafzai tribe living in northern Bajaur. They occupy areas that are green and fertile (for example, Nawagai and Charmang). Politically, the Salarzai, a branch of Tarkani, are the most influential because traditional ruling families belong to this clan.

The majority of Bajauris are **Uthmankhel**, also an offshoot of the Yousafzai tribe, living in southeastern Bajaur and parts of Mohmand. They own landlocked areas composed of barren hills and plains, leaving them less prosperous and more fragmented.

Mohmand tribesmen are known for their influence, power, and reputation as natural guerrilla fighters. One of the important themes among Mohmands is the description and details of the wars in which they took part. Known as a hardy and industrious tribe, Mohmands are generally preferred for jobs in some "settled areas" – especially in the neighboring NWFP districts of Charsadda, Mardan, and Peshawar, where many of them settled in the recent decades. Hence they are often called *doa-kora,* meaning "people with two homes." Within the Mohmand agency, Halimzai are considered the most important sub-tribe of Mohmands, as they control some strategic

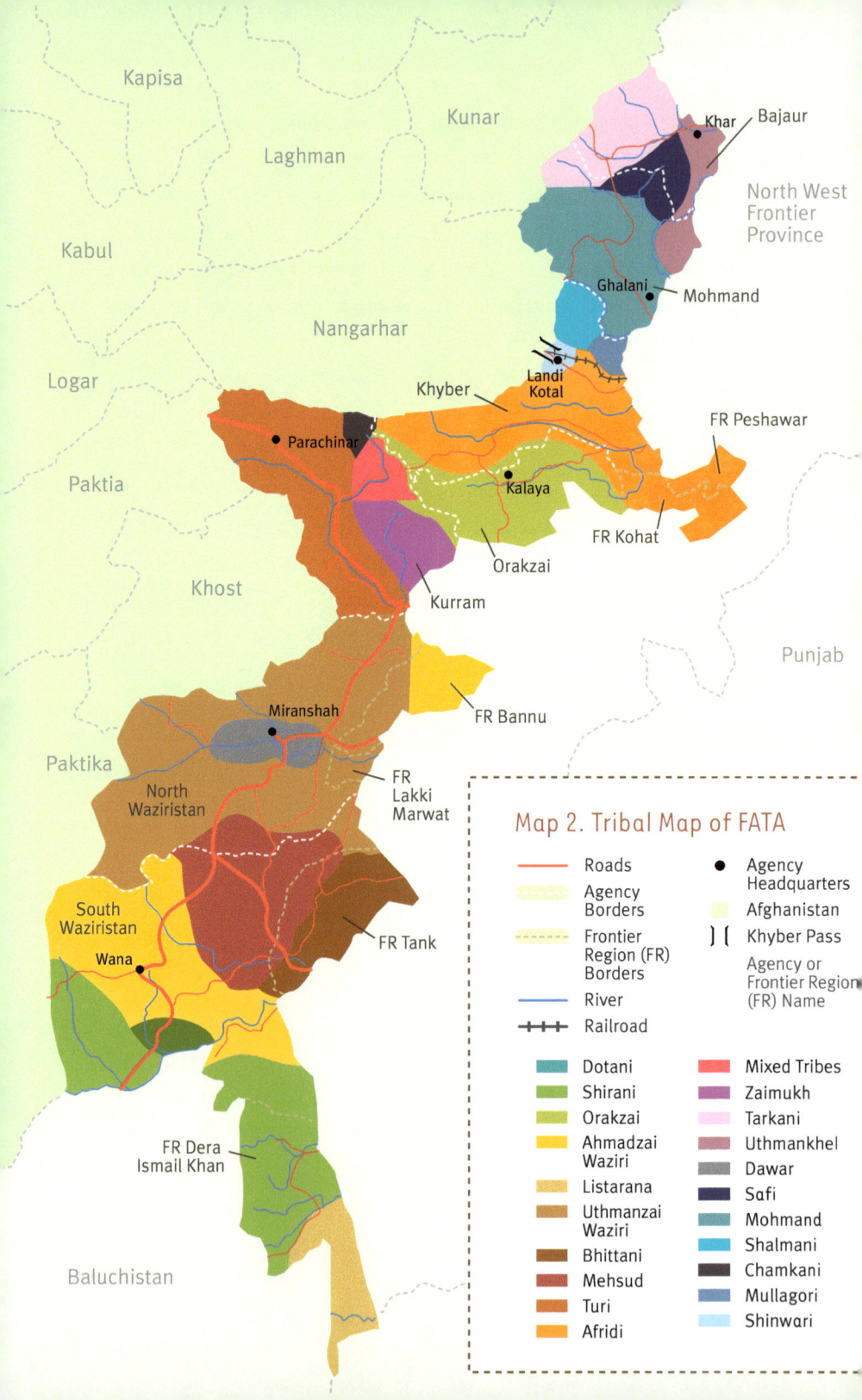

Kapisa

Kunar

Laghman

North West
Frontier
Province

Khar · Bajaur

Kabul

Nangarhar

Ghalani · Mohmand

Logar

Khyber

Landi
Kotal

FR Peshawar

Paktia

Parachinar

Kalaya

FR Kohat

Khost

Orakzai

Kurram

Punjab

FR Bannu

Miranshah

FR
Lakki
Marwat

Paktika

North
Waziristan

FR Tank

South
Waziristan

Wana

Map 2. Tribal Map of FATA

— Roads
● Agency Headquarters
Agency Borders
Afghanistan
Frontier Region (FR) Borders
) (Khyber Pass
— River
Agency or Frontier Region (FR) Name
╫ Railroad

Dotani	Mixed Tribes
Shirani	Zaimukh
Orakzai	Tarkani
Ahmadzai Waziri	Uthmankhel
Listarana	Dawar
Uthmanzai Waziri	Safi
Bhittani	Mohmand
Mehsud	Shalmani
Turi	Chamkani
Afridi	Mullagori
	Shinwari

FR Dera
Ismail Khan

Baluchistan

locations, including main routes, markets, and important passes. They are also in the majority in the area where the Mohmand head-quarters is located.

The **Safi** tribe lives mostly in the north-central part of the Mohmand agency close to Bajaur agency. Safis are known for their peaceful demeanor and loyalty to Pakistan. They are mostly involved in farming and the timber business. The Safi tribe also has a significant presence in southern Afghanistan.

Based in the Tirah area, the **Afridi** tribe is the most powerful and dominant tribe in Kyber agency. Afridis, the guardians of the Khyber Pass, are widely known throughout the region for their courageousness. From a different perspective, British historians remember them as a rebellious and treacherous tribe. While short-tempered, Afridis are known as good fighters who are pragmatic in picking their battles and making alliances. They respect Sufis and their shrines, which intellectually aligns them with Barelvi Sunnis, considered the rival of conservative and pro-Taliban Deobandi Sunni groups. The Afridi tribe has also produced great men of literature. This tribe is further divided into eight distinct clans: Adamkhel (located in the eastern part of the agency – Dara Adamkhel), Akakhel, Kamarkhel, Qamberkhel, Malik Dinkhel, Kukikhel, Zakhakhel, and Sepah.

Shinwaris, the second largest tribe of Khyber agency, are also influential, but members mostly live in Nangarhar province in Afghanistan. Their ability to influence politics on both sides of the Durand Line adds immensely to their power. They also enjoy excellent relations with Afridis, and there is no history of any serious rivalry between the two. They are largely involved in business activities and are well off. They are also well traveled and are especially considered experts in harvesting popular regional fruits both in Pakistan and Afghanistan.

Among the smaller tribes in Kyber agency, **Mullagoris** are relatively uneducated and poor. Living in the north of the agency, they own marble deposits in the area, but have not been able to set up any factories to refine marble. The **Shalmani**, a small tribe that resembles the Mohmand, is quiet and peaceful. It resides on the north side of the Khyber agency – closer to the Mohmand agency.

The origin of **Orakzai** tribe is shrouded in mystery. It is believed that a Persian prince named Sikandar Shah, who was exiled from his kingdom, took the name "Wrakzai" (also pronounced "orak zai," meaning "lost son"). According to folklore, he and his followers came to be known as Orakzais. This tribe is considered quite similar to Afridis in character and traits, and a few Orakzai sub-tribes are Shia. The Sunni and Shia communities are separated by a natural boundary, the Mastura River, with the Shia living on the river's south end. The Massuzai clan of the Orakzai has a long running, yet not currently very significant, feud with the Chamkani tribe, which borders them on the west in Kurram agency.

A small **Sikh** community also lives in the Orakzai agency, and they call themselves Pashtun and speak Pashto. The Sikh community belongs to the Punjab and Haryana provinces of India and are ethnically Punjabis. Sikhs ruled Punjab before 1849. They expanded their rule briefly to parts of NWFP and present-day FATA. Some Sikhs then moved to various parts of FATA.

Turis, the predominant tribe of Kurram agency, live in the Kurram Valley next to the western end of the Miranzai Valley. With Turkic origins, it is the only tribe that is almost completely Shia. Turis are known for their well-developed social and legal framework, and their body of customary law is called *Turizoona*. Turis also have very good relations with their neighboring tribes in Afghanistan. During their clashes with other tribes in FATA (mostly due to sectarian rifts and their anti-Taliban and anti-al-Qaeda activities), they use their access to Afghanistan for food and medical supplies. The Bangash tribe remained the uncontested masters of Kurram agency until the 18th century when the Turis (who basically were a nomadic tribe) attacked the area and secured their control. The Turi say they were reacting to an incident where a member of the Bangash tribe disgraced a Turi girl.

Many from the **Bangash** tribe are also Shia (especially those belonging to the Samilzai sub-tribe). They have Arab origins according to legend. The Shia Bangash live in Upper Kurram, but the Sunni Bangash reside in Lower Kurram. Turi and Bangash Shia are mostly supportive of the US/NATO operations in Afghanistan.

Zaimukh, a Sunni tribe that shifted to this area from Afghanistan, is notorious for feuds with all of its neighbors.

The **Uthmanzai Wazirs** dominate the hilly tracts of North Waziristan: Khaisora, Sherathala Plain, Kaitu Valley, lower stretches of the Kurram River, and upper parts of Tochi Valley. The Utmanzai Wazirs are known to be more rebellious than the other main tribe in North Waziristan: the Daur.

The **Daurs** (or Dawar) were depicted in British records as "the most fanatical and priest ridden race." They have settled in the fertile Tochi Valley, mostly on the left bank of the Tochi River. They are industrious agriculturalists, and their villages are strongly walled. In 1925, the neighboring Wazirs bought large areas of land from the Daurs in the Tochi Valley. As a result, the Daurs are surrounded by Waziris on all sides. The Daur are locally called "administered Wazir." Since the British years, they have been known for striking deals with whomever is powerful in the region. They have also been considered untrustworthy by other tribes in the area.

Considered by the British to be the most intractable of all tribes, the **Mehsuds** are divided into three main divisions – Alizai, Shabikhel, and Manzai – and accordingly named *Dre* (three) Mehsuds. The Mehsud tribe inhabits the northern regions of South Waziristan near Razmak (North Waziristan). Most of the areas where Mehsuds live are mountainous and they rely on the Burki tribe for their armaments. The principal villages of the Mehsuds are Makin and Kanigurram. Khanigurram is also inhabited by a tribe called Urmar of Indian descent – they have a language of their own called *Bargista*, but identify themselves with the Mehsud tribe.

The **Ahmadzai Wazirs** control the border regions between South Waziristan and Afghanistan. Their ancestral home appears to have been in the Birmal Valley of Afghanistan. Two-thirds of the Ahmadzais live in the Bannu district of NWFP and the remaining live in South Waziristan agency near Wana and the Shakai Valley. The Ahmadzai Wazirs have largely avoided destructive internal feuds, and they are known for their tribal unity.

Both Mehsuds and Ahmadzai Wazirs are proud to have a formidable reputation as warriors and are known for their frequent blood feuds. According to historian and British Governor of NWFP Sir Olaf Caroe, Mehsuds would never consider submitting to a foreign power that has entered their land. In his writings, he likens the Mehsuds to a wolf and the Wazir to a panther. They are reputed to be good marksmen and are known for their trustworthiness. They are also the most independent of all the tribes and have the highest literacy rate among Pashtuns of the region. While the area has produced many senior civil and military officers, the political leadership of South Waziristan is increasingly dominated by conservative clerics and a younger generation of radicals.

Some **Kuchi** settlers can be found in the southwest corner of South Waziristan between Thati and Zarmelan. The **Bhittanis** inhabit a strip of land along the southeast border of South Waziristan.

A tribal leaders fortified home in FATA. While officially governed by the President of Pakistan, the agencies are actually governed by tribes through a combination of maliks(leaders) and jirgas (councils).

PHOTO BY ANTHONY MAW

Chapter 4
Government and Leadership

O fficially governed by a confusing structure under the president of
Pakistan, FATA is actually ruled by the tribes and increasingly the
Taliban. FATA is an invention of colonial history. Its borders and somewhat
confusing power structures have been sustained from the independence
of Pakistan in 1947 to the emergence of the mujahedin and Taliban in the
modern era. Its creation recognized the undeniable independence of the
tribes in the 19th century, and that tradition remains a dominant feature
of FATA governance today. Official agency administrators and governing
bodies have waning influence and authority and are often intimidated by
Taliban militants.

ADMINISTRATIVE AND CONSTITUTIONAL
FRAMEWORK

According to Pakistan's 1973 constitution, FATA is included among the
"territories" of Pakistan that are separate from the four provinces of
Pakistan's federation. However, the power structures that govern FATA are
complex. Though represented in the National Assembly and the Senate
(universal suffrage was introduced in 1997), it remains under the direct
executive authority of the president. Laws legislated by Parliament do
not apply in FATA. Only the president is empowered to issue regulations

for the "peace and good government" of the tribal areas. In essence, FATA continues to be governed primarily through the Frontier Crimes Regulation of 1901. FATA is administered by the governor of the NWFP as an agent to the president. The administration of FATA is under the overall supervision of the Ministry of States and Frontier Regions in Islamabad. This ministry functions under the prime minister of the country, and hence the prime minister can indirectly influence developments in FATA. In actual practice, the governor of NWFP and the president together make the most important decisions in FATA. However, the inspector general of the Frontier Corps (FC) and the Corps Commander's IX Corps based in Peshawar have also had a direct role in FATA since the beginning of major military operations.

Until 2002, development issues in FATA were managed by the NWFP provincial planning and development department (FATA section). At the time a separate FATA Secretariat was set up, headed by the Secretary of FATA, to directly plan, monitor, and oversee development work in FATA. In 2006, a fully fledged civil secretariat of FATA was set up to take over decision-making functions and project implementation, with an additional chief secretary, four secretaries, and a number of directors. The NWFP governor's secretariat plays a coordinating role for interaction between the federal and provincial governments and the civil secretariat of FATA. On the ground, the Pakistani army's preferences also play a significant role.

The British navigated local customs and power centers in the 19th century by creating a system based on three institutions that mostly stand to this day: the political agent, the tribal elders, and the 1901 Frontier Crimes Regulation (FCR). The office of the political agent is at the center of the whole structure. In reality, political agents' capacity to initiate and implement governmental policy is waning. Political agents are also influenced by the priorities of senior army officers and ISI directives.

Table 3. Important Officials of FATA

NAME	DESIGNATION	CONTACT DETAILS
Habibullah Khan	Additional Chief Secretary, FATA Secretariat, Peshawar.	Tel: +92-91- 9212148 *hk654@yahoo.com*
Major Attaullah	Chief Executive, FATA Development Authority	Tel: +92-91-9218517 *ce@fatada.gov.pk*
Zafar Hasan	Secretary, Planning & Development Department, FATA Secretariat, Peshawar	Tel: +92-91-9212130 *zafar_h@hotmail.com*
Fakhar-e Alam	Director, General Projects FATA Secretariat, Peshawar	Tel: +92-91-9213015 *fakhrea2001@yahoo.co.uk*

Political Agents

Political Agents (PAs) administer each agency. They are senior appointed bureaucrats from federal or NWFP provincial administrative services who serve simulateously as the chief executive, judicial, and administrative office, and, under certain circumstances, revenue collector. Traditionally, the office of the PA extends state policy by commanding tribal and irregular forces (the *khassadars* and levies, as discussed below), and co-opting influential tribal elders. The PA's power is implicitly limited by having to balance the interests of various elders. The commissioner, a supervising authority, used to be the most direct check on the PA's power, but the post was scrapped in the 2002 Devolution Plan, an administrative reform project under President Pervez Musharraf. Concerns abound about the PA's centralized power, judicial involvement, and largely secret patronage funds. The PA is aided by assistant political agents (heads of sub-divisions), *tehsildars* (head of sub-unit Tehsil), and *moharrir* (clerks).

Maliki System

The second pillar is the *maliki* system. A malik is an influential elder who generally cooperates with the state. The title is hereditary, and regular benefits and subsidies are sometimes sanctioned for this system. *Lungi* system operates below the maliki setup. As former NWFP governor Iftikhar Hussain described it, "This system of nurturing local elites at the cost of discouraging voices of disagreement did suit the rulers of the past...[today] maliks jealously cut down to size anyone who tries to break the ranks." The PA of each agency has a security force consisting of *khassadara* (local police), levies, and scouts. Local tribes contribute men to the *khassadars* who protect roads and bridges, escort government officials, and help maliks execute government orders. The FC provides general security for the entire agency. Two concepts relevant to this system are:

Nikat: A distribution system through which the tribe shares all the benefits and losses. It is evaluated on the basis of their ancestral positions.

Majab: An allowance paid to a tribe (as a whole and on a case-by-case basis) in return for of its cooperation and loyalties.

Frontier Crimes Regulations (FCR)

The FCR of 1901 is the third pillar of this overall setup. The British initially extended civil and criminal laws in force elsewhere to the frontier districts. However, they enacted the first Frontier Crimes Regulation in 1871 due to the low rate of conviction. The current form was enacted in 1901. The FCR allegedly sought to encapsulate elements of the Pashtun tribal code, pashtunwali, and customs, such as the "trial" procedure of the jirga. Surveys suggest, however, that a majority of people in FATA believe the FCR only contains a negative exploitation of pashtunwali. Select FCR provisions violate fundamental rights enshrined in Pakistan's constitution, entailing harsh penalties, lack of due process, and a limited right to appeal. These provisions have led human rights activists to dub the FCR a "black law." Some such notorious penalties are: the power to blockade hostile or unfriendly tribes (section 21); demolition and restriction of construction of a hamlet, village, or town on the frontier (section 31); and removal of people from their places of residence (section 36).

Maliks make their decisions through a jirga, and PAs play an important role in the composition of a jirga. The jirga system is an indigenous conflict resolution mechanism developed in the area over centuries. In case of a dispute, both sides are listened to, and an authority of these parties (*waak*) is obtained. Both parties are then asked to deposit some rifles or guns as a surety, which also helps set up a ceasefire (*teega*). The right of appeal is available in some cases, at which point a new jirga is constituted. This rarely happens. The decision of the jirga is binding. To implement a decision, a jirga can constitute a *lashkar* (armed force), meant to be a representative force raised by taking one or two members of each household (or street).

Table 4. Political Agents of FATA

POLITICAL AGENT	AGENCY	PHONE NUMBER
Shafir Ullah	PA Bajaur agency	0942-220558 0942-220559
Amjid Ali Khan	PA Mohmand agency	0924-290001 0924-290002
Tariq Hayat	PA Khyber agency	09211901-5
Muhammad Baseer	PA Orakzai agency	0925-621542 0925-621543
Mohammad Azam Khan	PA Kurram agency	0926-310530 0926-310590
Mutaher Zeb	PA North Waziristan agency	0928-300798

A truck winds down the mountainside to the Khyber Pass carrying goods it will sell in Afghanistan. Instability and demographic change in the border region have transformed the economy of FATA, from one based on agriculture and pastoralism to one dependent on the unregulated, cross-border trade of goods, including drugs and arms.

PHOTO BY ANTHONY MAW

Chapter 5
The Economy

C onflict, political instability, and demographic changes in the Afghanistan-Pakistan region since late 1970s have transformed the economy of FATA and surrounding areas. Once based on subsistence agriculture and nomadic pastoralism, the economy now depends on the unregulated, cross-border trade of goods, including drugs and arms. Conflict and extremism have prevented outside investment and contributed to the flight of human capital.

The economy of the area depends on smuggling routes that exploit the Afghan Transit Trade Agreement, under which goods are imported duty-free into Pakistan for re-export to Afghanistan since Afghanistan has no port of its own. Many of these cheaper duty-free items are then illegally sold in Pakistan. In 2001, the World Bank estimated the value of such trade at nearly $1 billion per year. Economists believe it has doubled since then.

Besides smuggling and the drug trade, car theft rackets and the illegal sale of locally-made weapons also generate revenue for different groups. FATA's illegal trade practices have created a new economically powerful class with political ambitions. Such groups have moved their families to either Peshawar or Karachi (or even the United Arab Emirates), but their business operations are managed and run from within different parts of FATA.

With around three percent of the national population, FATA receives only about one percent of the national budget. Some comparisons are insightful in this sphere: the per capita development alloca- tion is roughly one-third of the national average and the per capita income in FATA is half of Pakistan's national average. Historically, international aid agencies and NGOs were strongly discouraged from working in the tribal belt, though, more recently, some local NGOs (many with foreign funding) have begun operating in FATA. According to a 2006 United States Institute of Peace report, the region had the country's highest emigration ratio even before the advent of insurgency and militancy a few years ago. The militancy and army offensives have further displaced tens of thousands of people and disrupted the trade and economy of the area. The unemployment rate is 60-80 percent, excluding migrant laborers.

Overall, FATA is engulfed in abject poverty which has decreased employment opportunities over the years. Lack of arable land, shortage of rainfall, and an absence of farm mechanization all nega- tively impact agricultural output. There are very few dams for water storage, and crops are grown where level land is available. Wheat and maize are the two main crops, followed by the cultivation of rice (in areas where water is available), barley, and mustard. Land use data from 2003–04 shows that seven percent of the total geographic area of FATA is cultivated, one percent remains uncultivated, and more than 82 percent of the land is not available for cultivation. This puts intense pressure on available farmland, which supports an average of 18 people per cultivated hectare and more than 40 people per irrigated hectare. Some 44 percent of farmland is under irrigated, with the remaining cultivated area relying entirely on rainfall.

Table 5. Land use (FATA, 2003-04)

LAND USE	AREA (HA)
Reported area	2,722,042
Cultivated area	199,530
Irrigated area	87,011
Current fallow	30,607
Forest area	46,202
Uncultivated area	2,468,512
Not available for cultivation	2,240,761

MINERAL RESOURCES IN FATA

Nineteen different mineral deposits have been identified in the tribal areas: copper, manganese, chromite, iron ore, lead, barite, soapstone, coal, gypsum, limestone, marble, dolomite, feldspar, quartz, silica san, bentonite, marl, emerald, and graphite. The total mineral production in the year 2004-05 stood at 12.73 million tons.

With its meager resources, the government failed to allocate the required funds for proper mineral exploration and development. Foreign investors shied away from this sector due to worsening security environment. Additionally, very little private investment has taken place in this sector, and needed technology for exploration is not accessible in the area. The national government routinely leases these mineral deposit areas as favors to influential tribes. Due to lack of technical know-how, tribesmen have been using outmoded methods of mineral extraction. For instance, the use of crude explosive in a non-technical way results in a loss of large quantities of minerals and erodes the minerals' value.

Table 6. Minerals by Agency

AGENCY	MINERALS
Bajaur	Marble, Manganese, Chromite, and Emerald
Mohmand	Marble, Chromite, Silica sand, dolomite, Manganese, Quartz, Feldspar, and Emerald
Khyber	Marble, Barite, Graphite, Soapstone, and Limestone
Orakzai	Coal and Iron Ore
Kurram	Soapstone, Coal, Marble, Magnesite, Barite, Iron Ore, and Lead
North Waziristan	Copper, Manganese, Chromite, Magnesite, Coal, and Granite (dimension stone)
South Waziristan	Copper, Chromite, Marble, and Granite

Source: FATA Development Authority, Peshawar, 2007

Annual Revenue from Minerals in FATA (1998-2008): http://fatada.gov.pk/revenue.php

The geological surveys of 85 percent of the tribal belt have revealed immense prospects of mineral exploration. From fiscal years 1995 to 2004, mineral production increased by 35 percent annually.

Marble and Granite

Huge reserves of highly valued white marble in Ziarat, Mohmand agency, gray marble in Bajaur, and other attractive colored marble in Mohmand, Khyber, Bajaur, Orakzai, Kurram, and Waziristan have been identified. In FATA, the marble quarrying/mining industry has provided jobs to an estimated 2,000 people.

Gems

Emerald and tourmaline have been found in North Waziristan. Unverifiable amounts of garnet and quartz have been found in Bajaur and South Waziristan.

Table 7. Production of Minerals in 2003-04 (Quantity in Tons)

AGENCY	LIME STONE	MARBLE	COAL	SOAP STONE	QUARTZ	MANGANESE	CHROMATE	FLUORITE	SCRAP
Bajaur	130	18,973	-	282	-	90	-	-	-
Mohmand	-	543,749	-	2,360	29,759	-	3,377	-	279
Khyber	453,932	7,092	-	2,370	-	-	-	-	-
Orakzai	-	-	142,725	-	-	-	-	-	-
Kurram	-	-	35,505	-	-	-	-	90	-
North Waziristan	32	705	140	-	-	-	31,830	-	-
South Waziristan	-	-	-	-	-	-	-	-	-
Total:	**454,094**	**570,519**	**178,370**	**5,012**	**29,759**	**90**	**35,207**	**90**	**279**

Source: Mineral concession cell FATA secretariat, Peshawar

Copper

In North Waziristan, estimated reserves of 35 million tons have been discovered. Confirmed reserves of eight million tons have an average copper content of 0.8 percent.

Coal

FATA has an abundance of high quality coal deposits. Coal mining is currently very limited and uses old and outdated mining techniques. Huge deposits of coal have been found in Darra Adam Khel (Frontier Region Kohat), Orakzai, Kurram, and North Waziristan.

Soapstone

Soapstone is a metamorphic rock rich in magnesium and iron. FATA has huge deposits of soapstone (mostly in Kurram agency) that are used in local industry and exported. Currently the soapstone at Ghandhao is mined and exported to Europe.

INDUSTRY

Industrial activity in FATA is mostly restricted to small private-sector units that operate without any government involvement (in terms of registration, tax collection, safety measures, etc.). According to the Directorate of Industries of the FATA Secretariat, 1,082 industrial parks were operating in 2007 in the whole of FATA. Of these, 120 are located in Bajaur agency, 200 in Darra Adam Khel (where poor quality, cheap weapons are produced), 207 in Khyber agency, 28 in Kurram agency, 130 in Mohmand agency, 31 in North Waziristan, and 16 in South Waziristan. The remaining units are based in the Frontier Regions. These industrial units mostly relate to mineral extraction, food items, local craftwork, tailoring/clothing, and construction materials. However, no official or specific information about these businesses is available.

AGENCY-SPECIFIC ECONOMIC INDICATORS

Bajaur Agency

Extensive deposits of marble are found in several places throughout Bajaur agency. The marble is associated with the calcareous rocks, and the marble is processed there in different green and black colors. People in the Bajaur also live off of farming, small-scale business, and wages from daily labor jobs mostly in Khar or Timergara.

Mohmand Agency

Sources of income are limited in Mohmand, except in agriculture and some trade. Many residents have moved to Karachi (Sindh) or the Gulf States to work.

Khyber Agency

Because of its proximity to Peshawar and the direct road to Afghanistan, Khyber has many opportunities for traders and trans-porters. Most transporters in FATA live in Khyber. Many from this agency have also moved to Middle East for jobs. The timber trade is a major business, but it leads to deforestation and attendant economic problems. People in Khyber largely depend on Peshawar to supply daily necessities. In the remote areas of Khyber agency, livestock and dry fruit are the main sources of income. People in these areas grow vegetables that are sold throughout FATA and NWFP. Khyber also benefits from being the only source of limestone in FATA; 4.6 million tons were extracted in 2008.

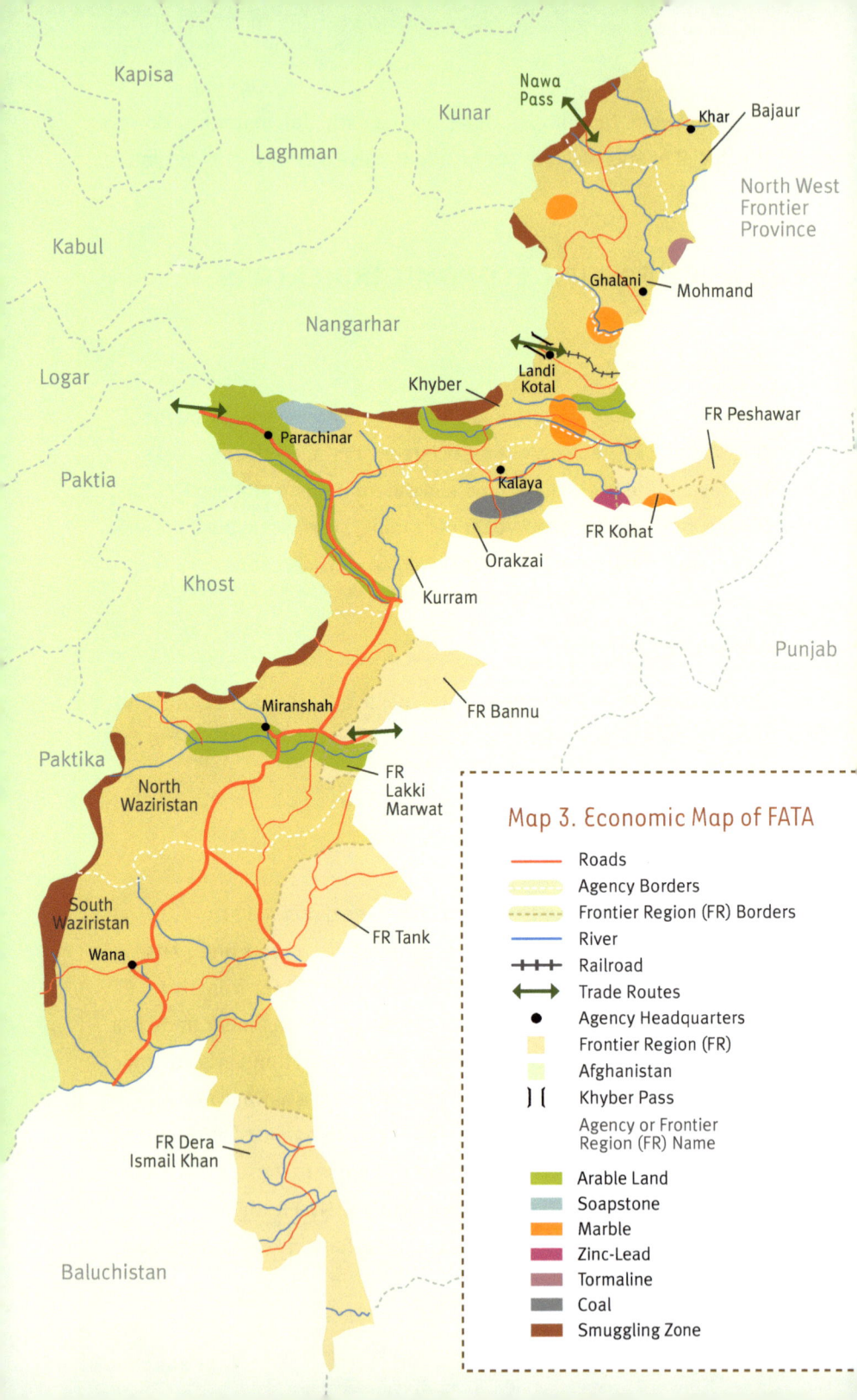

Map 3. Economic Map of FATA

Legend:
- Roads
- Agency Borders
- Frontier Region (FR) Borders
- River
- Railroad
- Trade Routes
- Agency Headquarters
- Frontier Region (FR)
- Afghanistan
- Khyber Pass
- Agency or Frontier Region (FR) Name
- Arable Land
- Soapstone
- Marble
- Zinc-Lead
- Tormaline
- Coal
- Smuggling Zone

Labels on map:
Kapisa, Kunar, Nawa Pass, Khar, Bajaur, North West Frontier Province, Laghman, Kabul, Nangarhar, Ghalani, Mohmand, Logar, Khyber, Landi Kotal, FR Peshawar, Parachinar, Paktia, Kalaya, FR Kohat, Orakzai, Khost, Kurram, Punjab, FR Bannu, Miranshah, FR Lakki Marwat, Paktika, North Waziristan, South Waziristan, Wana, FR Tank, FR Dera Ismail Khan, Baluchistan

Orakzai Agency

In the recent past, reserves of coal have been found in various areas of Orakzai, including Sheikhan, Mishti, and Feroz Khel areas. Presently, ill-qualified private contractors are exploiting the coal deposits. Local parties use primitive methods to carry out small-scale mining. About 10,000 tons of coal are excavated per month. Development potential for proper mining exists in a region covering more than 1,600 square kilometers. Most of the tribesmen are engaged in agriculture and animal husbandry. Many of the educated families from the area moved to urban centers of NWFP in the past few decades. Some of the senior bureaucrats and armed forces personnel are originally from this agency.

Kurram Agency

The worsening local Shia-Sunni conflict, the Taliban blockade of the agency since mid-2007, and other military operations have adversely affected Kurram's economy. As a result, Kurram agency receives its food supply and other necessities from neighboring Afghanistan. Diminished security and a correlated decline in local transportation are increasing food prices and construction and transportation costs, sometimes dramatically. Prior to military operations in the area, the travel cost between Peshawar and Parachinar (Kurram agency) was Rs. 200 (US $2.50) per person; it is now more than Rs.5,000 (US $60) per person, as the people of Kurram agency have to travel via Afghanistan because other transit routes are closed. Soapstone can be found in the eastern extreme of the Safed Koh and the upper parts of Daradar Valley. However, mining and excavation activities related to the marble industry have stopped due to the security environment, creating more distress for the local economy.

South Waziristan

The majority of Wazirs and Mehsuds of South Waziristan are pastoral. The Wazirs breed a good race of horses and sheep, often earning their livelihood from sheep rearing. Many Mehsuds are employed in the army as levies and *khassadars*. Mehsuds run commercial buses and trucks out of Tank and Dera Ismail Khan. Charcoal, wool, potatoes, chilghozas (a dry fruit), and a few varieties of locally grown fruits are traded in South Waziristan. This agency also makes small arms and knives, known for their artistic finishes. Coal mines have been discovered in recent years in the area of Neeli Kach Tehsil (near Wana), and copper reserves are found in Preghal and Spin Kamar.

North Waziristan

North Waziristan's economy is very similar to that of South Waziristan. Copper reserves at Boya and Manzarkhel Spinkamar (east of Shora-Algad) are potentially an important source of trade and income, but development of these locations remains in limbo due to the security situation. In some hilly areas of the agency, ordinary stones are mined for local construction of buildings as well as for construction in other parts of FATA.

SMUGGLING THROUGH DURAND LINE

FATA is the major transit route for large-scale smuggling operations from Afghan territory into Pakistan, and vice versa. The Durand Line is far more apparent on printed maps than it is on the ground, and local populations have never paid much attention to the border. It runs through a rugged and arid mountainous region inhabited by subsistence farmers living in scattered villages. It is poorly demarcated in most places, and not demarcated at all in others. Understanding the difference between a boundary and a frontier is important in this situation. An international boundary marks a separation (natural or artificial) between two contiguous states. A frontier is the portion of a territory that faces the border of another country, including both the boundary line itself and the land contiguous to it.

Some villages in Pakistan have their farmland in Afghanistan, and vice versa. Historically, the Pakistani and Afghan governments recognized this fact by not demanding papers from local people even at formal border crossings. This practice has changed since 2002. One example quoted by an expert at a 2007 Boston University seminar on the Durand Line maintained that that about half the population of the Pakistani border town of Chaman on the road to Qandahar (in the Baluchistan province adjacent to FATA) crosses the border daily into Afghanistan. This includes the Afghan police employed at the Spin Boldak border crossing a kilometer away who commute to their post from homes in Pakistan.

There used to be only two official trade links between Pakistan and Afghanistan: Torkham (Khyber Pass, Peshawar-Kabul) and Weish (Bolan Pass, Quetta-Kandahar). Now there are over 20, including unofficial places of trade through shingle roads and tracks on which trucks, minibuses, and pickups operate frequently. Achakzais, Waziris, Turis, Shinwaris, and Mohmands have relatives on both sides of the border. Only Afridis and Mehsuds do not have kinship on the Afghanistan side. Arms trafficking, drugs trafficking, and smuggling of household commodities are the biggest sources of income in these areas.

According to a Pakistani military strategist, about 249 unfrequented routes along the Durand Line were not guarded at all times, but Pakistan also has 665 checkpoints along the Durand Line to check for smuggling and insurgents (2006-07 figures). Given the area's topography and relations between the tribes across the frontier, there are probably not enough checkpoints to sufficiently curb smuggling and insurgent movements.

A washed-out road. Under the FCR, FATA pays no taxes. Given scarce budgetary resources, Pakistan has always shied away from investing in FATA's infrastructure, depriving the area and its people of needed economic development.

PHOTO BY ANTHONY MAW

Chapter 6
Infrastructure and
International Assistance

F ATA remains the most underdeveloped area of Pakistan, and
its infrastructure does not adequately support the needs of its
people. Without financial resources from the national government,
private sector investment, or international donors, FATA's people stay
isolated and disconnected from the rest of Pakistan.

Development in FATA has historically been carried out in a compart-
mentalized fashion, concentrating narrowly around specific sectors.
This ad hoc approach has largely benefited local elites, depriving large
segments of the population of economic and social infrastructure. Many
projects in the tribal areas lack oversight, impact, and sustainability. For
example, many donors provide funds directly to the national government
for disbursement to local NGOs, but most foreign donors do not have
field offices to monitor any reforms that they are financing. Absence of
reliable statistical data is another issue because there has not been a
census in Pakistan recently. Government figures are often unreliable and
contradictory, making the job of planners much more difficult. Another
disincentive for private-sector investment is the customary requirement in FATA that any prospective business owner or investor who is an
"outsider" must first sign a contract with the tribe that resides in the

area. No courts exist in FATA. In case of conflict, one has to rely on the judgment of a local jirga.

INFRASTRUCTURE

Roads: According to the Pakistan Census Report 1998, there are a total of 4,428 kilometers of roads in FATA (2,500 of which are "high type" while 1,928 are of "low type" – reflecting quality).

Communications: There are six telegraph offices and 46 telephone exchanges in FATA. Mobile phones function only in some parts of FATA: Khyber agency, North Waziristan (in areas closer to the NWFP districts, especially closer to Tank district), Bajaur agency (closer to Malakand district), and Kurram agency (closer to Hangu district border). Even in these areas, signals are better in the hills facing NWFP. Mobile service was made available by Mobilink, Pakistan's largest cellular company, in South Waziristan in March 2009. The official website of Mobilink mentions the following areas where mobile service is available:

- **Upper Kurram, Parachinar:** Upper Kurram Parachinar, Shablen, Sadda, Manden, Mandari, Ahmadishama, Ali Zai, Chapri.

- **Bajaur agency:** Zor Bandar, Yousaf Abad, Sadiq Abad Phatak, Qazafi Tehsil, Loay Sam, Khar Bajur, Barkhaloz, Gulushah, Inayat Kili, Jar Bajaur.

- **Mohmand agency:** Parang Ghar, Ghalanay.

- **Khyber agency:** Sur Kummar, Sultan Khel, Sheikhmal Khel, Rupa Khasadar, Mukhtiar Khel, Bara, Landi Kotal, Khughkhel, Khuga Khel, Jamrud, Haji Abdullah Jan Kalay.

[For updates of mobile phones coverage area in FATA see: *www.mobilinkgsm.com/coverage/coverage_map.php*]

Education: There are 2,567 primary schools, 278 middle schools, 201 high schools, and nine colleges (all colleges are for male students only). Around 800 community schools (in households) and 200 mosque schools are also operational. According to government records from 2007, a total of 519,060 students (366,797 male and 152,263 female) are enrolled in educational institutions. The total number of teachers in FATA's public education system is 18,895 (13,448 male and 5,447 female). As the security in FATA has worsened, these numbers have declined, but no credible estimates are available. In 2005-06 the Asian Development Bank funded $2 million directed toward building science laboratories. Larger grants from USAID and Japan of about $5 million each have helped the education facilities in the area. However, only 40 percent of school-aged children are estimated to be enrolled. The figures are worse for girls, with only 21 percent enrolled. Among these, about 50 percent drop out by the time they reach fifth grade.

Health Sector: There are 41 hospitals, 190 dispensaries, five rural heath units, six tuberculosis clinics, 16 mother and child health centers, 167 basic health units, and eight other health centers. Some private clinics are also operational in FATA. Wealthier patients are brought to major hospitals in Peshawar for serious diseases and surgeries. According to the World Health Organization, 135 out of every 1,000 children under the age of five in FATA die from curable illnesses. Also, around 60 percent of child deaths in FATA are attributed to water- and sanitation-related diseases. There is one hospital bed for every 2,179 people in FATA, compared to one for every 1,341 in Pakistan as a whole. There is one doctor for every 7,670 people compared to one doctor per 1,300 people in Pakistan as a whole. This meager health infrastructure came under severe stress when extremists aligned with al-Qaeda and the Taliban banned the polio vaccine, claiming that it is a Western ploy to decrease population growth. In response, many doctors and medical staff were attacked for continuing to vaccinate children.

Clean Drinking Water: According to official records, 56 percent of people have access to drinking water, but less than one third of this supply is in the form of individual connections to households. In many areas, women are required to travel two to three kilometers to fetch water. Sanitation facilities are available to less than ten percent of the population.

Housing: About 36 percent of houses are built with cement, less than 60 percent have access to electricity, and under two percent have access to natural gas.

Banking Sector: Six different banks operate 47 branches across FATA, some of which have been destroyed in the recent conflict. The national government does not let these banks to loan money to people in FATA, although the loans are allowed in other parts of the country. The absence of a robust legal framework to regulate financial services and commercial transactions makes the business climate uncertain.

DEVELOPMENT WORK IN FATA

Some residents of FATA believe the distribution of development funds has been uneven. Politically influential leaders can divert resources toward their towns, creating further disappointment and frustration among ordinary people. Furthermore, the few local NGOs in the area have left due to violence.

FATA Development Authority

In light of the area's dismal development indicators, FATA Development Authority (FATA DA) was set up as a semi-autonomous body in September 2006. This organization is responsible for the preparation and execution of development programs, projects, and trade and industry plans, industrial infrastructure and estates, and the development of mineral resources in FATA. It has its own board of directors that is fully empowered to make all major decisions. Members are drawn from the private sector and civil society. The authority works on commercial lines and acts like a corporate body. The government is keen to see FATA DA work quickly to develop natural and human resources in FATA.

Small Dams

Traditionally, natural springs and the construction of temporary diversions to the water flow irrigated small patches of land along sreams. However, the water table depleted in the region due to water waste and unbalance withdrawals of sub-surface water. Two small storage reservoirs were constructed recently: one at Talai in Bajaur agency and the other one at Milward in the Khyber agency. This covers an area of about 525 acres. Five other small dams – Maidani Dam and Kot Ragh in Kurram agency, Mir Kalam and Mersi Khel in North Waziristan agency, and Kharoshah Dam in Bajaur agency – are in various stages of completion under the supervision of the FATA Secretariat. These five small dams will irrigate a total of about 2,400 acres of land. Government consultants have identified an additional 120 potential dam sites, but not much progress has been made thus far.

In 2007-08 FATA DA initiated two projects in Dargai Pal in South Waziristan and another at Dandy in North Waziristan. These two projects will irrigate 1,123 acres and 2,000 acres, respectively. Another dam project in the Bara area of Khyber agency is expected to commence in late 2009. This dam will also generate about 5.8 MW of power. However, the militancy in FATA (especially in South Waziristan, North Waziristan, and Bajaur) has become so acute that no official of the FATA Development Authority or FATA Secretariat can go there to monitor the progress of development works.

Development work responsibilities are divided between the FATA Secretariat and FATA DA. The secretariat looks after education, health sector, water supply and sanitation, rural development, agriculture and livestock, forest and fisheries, irrigation, water management and power, roads and bridges, and institutional strengthening. The FATA DA is responsible for minerals, small dams, industries, skill development, township development, and tourism.

Reconstruction Opportunity Zones (ROZ)

The concept of ROZ is to develop industrial parks that offer international-standards in infrastructure, facilities, and incentives to attract national and international investment to set up modern industrial units with the guarantee and safety of investment. ROZs aim to promote investment and employment in economically deprived areas that lead to regional economic growth, and thus stability and security. All products made and processed in ROZs would be eligible for duty-free access to the United States. The concept of ROZs is similar to Qualifying Industrial Zones (QIZs) set up in Egypt and Jordan. Existing incentives and regulatory structures for Export Processing Zones (like free trade zones) in Pakistan are offered to ROZs.

USAID Projects

USAID is also working on a comprehensive program to support short-, medium-, and long-term objectives of the national government's FATA Sustainable Development Plan (FSDP) for 2006-2015. USAID's objectives include enhancing the government's legitimacy in FATA, improving economic and social conditions for local communities, and supporting sustainable development. To achieve the objectives, USAID expanded its earlier program and initiated new activities including: building the capacity of FATA institutions to deliver services to citizens, improving livelihoods, strengthening health and education services, and developing FATA's infrastructure. However, work has been temporarily stopped at 25 USAID-managed projects in FATA since early 2009 due to the deteriorating security situation in FATA. Locals working with foreign-funded programs in the region are increasingly being targeted by the Taliban and like-minded groups.

Since 2003, USAID's $254.6 million health program has focused on improving maternal, newborn, and child health care; enhancing the accessibility of family planning services; preventing the spread of infectious diseases; increasing access to safe drinking water; and strengthening key institutions in Pakistan's health sector.

Marble City in Mohmand Agency

In order to process the available marble into products compatible in the international market, a "marble city" is being set up in Mohmand agency through a public sector plan. An area of 300 acres has been acquired and handed over to Pakistan Stone Development Company Islamabad (PASDEC) for development. Around 200 units will be set aside for refining marble. According to the official spearheading the planning and construction of this area, almost 85 percent of marble in Pakistan is wasted due to conventional blasting and lack of proper facilities.

Focused Development – Model Villages

In recent years, the national government has used foreign funding to upgrade water and sanitation in 20 model villages in Khyber and Mohmand agencies (out of a total of 3,000 villages in FATA). The goal is to motivate communities toward self-financed, small, and local business ventures. In a similar effort, a recreational park was constructed in Bajaur agency. Earlier, fisheries development was supported in Kurram and

Orakzai agencies to assist the local community's effort to develop small businesses and popularize fish farming.

Important Infrastructure Projects in FATA

Warsak Dam: Warsak Hydro Power station is situated on the Kabul River about 32.2 km from Peshawar. The construction of the project was started in 1955, and the power station was commissioned in 1960.

Munda Dam: Munda Dam is being constructed on Swat River to the east of the agency. The national government is the main beneficiary of these dams. Private businesses also use electricity generated from the dams. The dams are heavily guarded by the security forces and have not been targeted by militants.

New Steel Bridges: Most of FATA's roads pass through mountainous terrain where flash floods are very common. The floods wash up large boulders and other debris, which render the roads unpassable. Though roads exist, many areas become inaccessible in such conditions. Therefore, the government decided to build 15 steel bridges in 2006 to help move military and civilian traffic. The army's Engineer Corps was tasked to build these bridges with a cost of $6.5 million provided by the US government. Most of these bridges are located in Mohmand, Khyber, and Kurram agencies.

Power: Tribal Electric Supply Company (TESCO) was formed in 2002 after separating from NWFP's electricity supply system. It manages the electricity supply to FATA. About 60 percent of all households have electricity, but low voltage and frequent and prolonged breakdowns are serious issues. A systematic effort to collect fees for electricity has largely failed, with 98 percent of customers paying nothing. In Khyber agency a micro-hydro approach is working. Sixty-seven small hydropower units, each with a capacity of 6 kW, have been handed over to villagers for operation and maintenance (with very basic training).

Pakistan-Afghanistan Trade

According to a United States Institute of Peace (USIP) study, nearly half of today's Afghan population has visited Pakistan at some point, making it the country that Afghans are most familiar with outside their homeland. About 60,000 Pakistanis currently work in Afghanistan, and 10,000 of them cross the border daily. Pakistan's exports to Afghanistan grew from $221 million in 2001 to $1.2 billion in 2006, though they have declined in recent years due to security issues. The informal trade is thought to be about double this figure. US Trade and Development Agency, together with the Planning Commission of Pakistan and the Ministry of Finance of Afghanistan, signed a Memorandum of Understanding (MOU) in May 2009 agreeing to pursue a Pakistan-Afghanistan Infrastructure and Trade Initiative. The plan seeks to foster economic development in the two countries and promote trade with Afghanistan and other regional partners.

A checkpoint in Khyber manned by a member of the Khyber Rifles, a para-military force forming part of the Frontier Corps. Pakistan has largely neglected security in FATA, instead tasking the Frontier Corps with border security and law enforcement. While their tribal links bind them closely to the locals, members are known to desert when asked to take action against members of their own tribe.

PHOTO BY ANTHONY MAW

Chapter 7
Security Issues

Pakistan's FATA has emerged as a base of support both to the Taliban resurgence in Afghanistan and the rise of Tehrik-e Taliban Pakistan (Pakistani Taliban Movement or TTP). One reason the government failed to maintain control of most of FATA is that the power has gradually shifted away from the maliks to a new breed of religious radicals who are far less committed to Pakistan. The breakdown of the traditional authority of maliks started in 1980 when religious clerics united the tribes against the Soviet Union in Afghanistan. Maliks have been marginalized ever since. FATA was, and still is, the platform for Pakistan-based militant training. The rise of the Taliban in Afghanistan (1994-95), many of whose leaders were former refugees educated in Pakistani seminaries (madrassas), also greatly benefited from the cadres of Pakistani madrassa students who moved toward Kabul from FATA. The Pakistani Taliban were inspired by the gains of the Afghan Taliban, and several hundreds from FATA joined their movement under the leadership Mullah Muhammad Omar.

The situation deteriorated further when many Pakistani militant groups that were groomed by the country's intelligence agencies to operate in Indian-controlled Kashmir (in support of the local insurgency there) also moved their militant training camps to FATA after the 9/11 attacks. Previously, they had shifted some of their infrastructure to Afghanistan, which they used as a sanctuary during Taliban era. Some of these groups (e.g. Harkat ul-Mujahedin) developed working relationships with al-Qaeda in Afghanistan.

As noted earlier, law and order deteriorated after Pakistan failed to prevent the flow of escaping Taliban and al-Qaeda fighters into South Waziristan and Bajaur in 2001-2002. The Pakistani military move into FATA in 2003-04 was seen by tribesmen as a violation of the 1947 understanding on FATA's autonomy. This led to the recent rise in a government-TTP conflict in northwest Pakistan.

Relations between FATA residents and Pakistani security forces are in decline. In addition to the issues of violence, relations are strained because FATA residents are not adequately represented in Pakistan's armed forces. FATA residents also complain that army officers often fill senior command positions in the Frontier Corps, denying promotions to qualified FATA officers.

PAKISTAN SECURITY FORCES IN FATA

Pakistan's 550,000-man army is oriented toward a conventional war with India – not a counterinsurgency fight in the tribal areas. Until recently, the army largely stayed clear of FATA, leaving security to the Frontier Corps. The British colonial rulers developed the Frontier Corps (FC) as a tribal paramilitary force that provides border security and law enforcement. The FC is led and commanded by officers from the regular Pakistani army, but oversight of the organization rests with the Ministry of the Interior. Their tribal links and connections bind them strongly to the inhabitants of FATA, and they are familiar with the local dialect, people, and tribes. However, they sometimes desert when ordered to take action against members of their own tribe. An estimated 120,000 army and 50,000 FC troops are currently deployed in NWFP and FATA.

Khasadars and levies are in charge of law enforcement in FATA. These are locals who are appointed through the malik system. They are lightly armed and are supposed to guard roads and provide safe passage to travelers. They are not properly equipped with modern weapons, communication equipments, transport, accommodation, etc. to effectively face the well-funded and well-equipped militants and criminal elements. The total strength of the khasadars is about 17,000 while the number of levies personnel is 4,000 – highly insufficient to support the local administration in FATA. In 2007 and 2008, maliks moved to raise tribal *lashkars* (traditional militias) to implement state policies in Bajaur agency and Khyber agency. Militants saw this as a serious threat, and they attacked some jirgas that were constituted to raise lashkars. The potential danger of this strategy is that the leaders of these government-equipped lashkars may become independent local warlords later.

Funding for security forces in FATA is a problem. The average Pakistani earns Rs. 10,000 (US $125). Army soldiers in Pakistan earn about Rs. 8,000 (US $100) and receive benefits including healthcare and lodging. According to credible media reports, Taliban militants are paid Rs. 12,000 by their leadership. However, FATA security forces, including the FC and malik-appointees, are paid a meager monthly salary of around Rs. 4,000 (US $50). Pakistan has also received funds from the US for the reform and upgrade of the FC since 2007-08. A total of US $750 million will be disbursed for this purpose. These funds are being used for training and modernization of FC.

Pakistan's Inter-Service Intelligence (ISI) agency has an entangled and controversial role with FATA militants. ISI channeled funds (from the CIA and Saudi Arabia) to different militant groups in the tribal areas during the Soviet invasion of Afghanistan – some of these with a focus on liberating Kashmir from India, others with a direct interest in Afghanistan. The Taliban is the most notable of this second group. Around 2001, Musharraf decided to change government policy and no longer supported the Taliban. This change directly impacted the ISI, which had developed strong ties to members of the Taliban during their 30-year alliance.

Some Pakistani analysts and media report that elements of ISI or former ISI continue to support the Taliban. The extent of and authorization for this support is disputed. The Pakistani government denies the reports. Evidence suggests that ISI involvement ranges from retired ISI operatives assisting the Taliban to Pakistan rounding up high-level Taliban targets in a short amount of time – such as in Quetta in February 2007. The ease of the arrests suggested to US officials that while no covert support of the Taliban may exist, the ISI and Pakistani army have not made a concerted effort to eradicate them either. It may be the case that many individual agents continue to support the Taliban, while others work to eradicate the Taliban. Some international experts assert that the insurgency in FATA could not have reached the proportions it has without support or acquiescence from within the official military circles in Pakistan. These officials may distinguish between "good Taliban," who check Indian influence in Afghanistan and thus serve their traditional interests, and "bad Taliban," who are involved in attacks on the Pakistani Army and FC forces.

THE TALIBAN

There are an estimated 75,000-100,000 Taliban insurgents in FATA, representing about two percent of the population. Another 15-20 percent of the population sympathize with the Taliban, and about 75-80 percent of FATA can be considered conservative and anti-Western. In terms of total armed men, almost every Pashtun has a weapon, and there is widespread animosity toward Pakistani forces and NATO/US forces across the border. Although they are only a small percentage of the population, Taliban militants are systematically expanding their influence and control through a combination of an effective media and propaganda campaign and violence. Taliban insurgents use good communications and light weapons systems to terrorize the ordinary people into submission, eliminate those who resist, and enforce a dogmatic version of sharia law.

Taliban insurgents are organized in loose militias (without any rank or uniform) around personalities such as Baitullah Mehsud and Maulvi Nazir. Tribal affiliations play a crucial role. For example, the majority of Baitullah Mehsud's group is from the Mehsud tribe. According to Pakistan's Federal Investigation Agency's (FIA) investigations, most suicide bombers who targeted different places in Punjab and Islamabad belonged to the Mehsud tribe. Similarly, Maulvi Nazir, a member of the Wazir tribe, has attracted Waziris. However, Punjabi Taliban (those associated with *jihadi* groups in Punjab) who travel to FATA areas regularly are organized differently – in small cells and groups of 15-20 members.

Al-Qaeda support and influence may be on the rise among Taliban members. The propaganda materials used by the Taliban in the Pashto language are translations of Arabic-language al-Qaeda materials in many cases. Similarly, Taliban violence and intimidation are increasingly justified by *fatwas* (religious edicts) issued by many extremist religious figures declaring that army soldiers killed in encounters with tribal militias are not *shaheeds* (martyrs).

In most recent events, militants belonging to anti-Shia groups from Punjab have targeted the Shia community in the Kurram agency. Shia-Sunni conflict in Kurram increased, and its impact also reached Orakzai agency, where Shia-Sunni relations were historically tense. In the latest Taliban attacks, the homes and families of leading members of the ruling Awami National Party (ANP) in the NWFP are being targeted to discourage them from taking strong policy decisions against militants.

The Failure of the "Deal" Approach

The peace agreements between the Pakistani government and Taliban militias – Shakai Agreement (2004), Sra Rogha Agreement (2005), Miranshah Agreement (2006), Khyber Agreements (2008) – failed to deliver the desired results because these agreements were signed from a weak position, no monitoring and enforcement mechanisms were in place in case of violations, important stakeholders were neglected, the civil administrative structure was circumvented, and the negotiation process was mainly a militant-military affair. Not surprisingly, the peace agreements proved to be only a brief respite between rounds; the warring sides recouped, regrouped, and renewed fighting after a breathing space.

Extremist and Taliban Emergence in Swat and the Impact on FATA

The 2008 emergence of extremist Islamic opposition in Swat Valley of NWFP has had a critical impact in turning the government's attention toward the risks of extremism in the border areas. During 2008, Islamic militants in Swat under Sufi Mohammad and his son Fazlullah grew in strength and drew closer links with Taliban militants in FATA. Murder and kidnapping became a daily routine in 2008. The government did little, while local law enforcement and civil administration were overwhelmed. The Human Rights Commission of Pakistan's May 2009 report indicated instances where the army and ISI used their influence to save Fazlullah and his collaborators from local police. Military action began in the area later in 2008, but the situation remained tense.

Late in 2008, a "peace deal" was arranged with the understanding that Mohammad would disarm his cadres and bring Fazlullah to the mainstream. The project failed in the first few months of 2009 after Mohammad made extremist statements challenging the democratic government and vowed to expand sharia law from Swat throughout Pakistan. Fazlullah's group refused to give up arms. The government responded with a major military operation in the beginning of May 2009. Hundreds of TNSM and TTP militants were killed and arrested, and a major humanitarian crisis erupted due to the fighting. Until June 2009, about three million people from Swat, Buner, and Dir were displaced.

The Pakistani army conducted simultaneous operations in Dir in the southwest and Buner in the east, while Special Services Group (SGG) commandos blocked the Taliban's fallback area toward the north in Peochar Valley. Mingora City and Saidu Sharif area saw major urban battles. As of June 2009, the army was winning the conflict. Public and political support strengthened the military leadership's ability to take decisive action. The army's integrity and counterinsurgency skills will be tested by the speed with which they can defeat the Taliban in Swat. Military success in the Swat would help expand the government's writ in FATA. It is believed that TTP is carrying out suicide attacks in major cities of Pakistan to deter military and political leadership from expanding this strategy into FATA.

KEY MILITANT LEADERS IN FATA

Baitullah Mehsud

Regarded as the most powerful and dangerous Taliban commander in FATA, Baitullah Mehsud resides in South Waziristan and leads the Pakistani Taliban. His supporters have a presence in all seven FATA agencies, with an estimated militia of 8,000–10,000. He directly manages militant training camps in South Waziristan. He conceded on more than one occasion that he was indeed sending his men to wage jihad against US, NATO, and Afghan forces in Afghanistan. He has also routinely attacked Pakistani army deployments and is believed to be responsible for ordering many suicide attacks in major urban centers of Pakistan. His top associates include Waliur Rahman, who could succeed him in case of his death, and Qari Hussain, known for his expertise in training and deploying suicide bombers.

Gul Bahadur

A direct descendant of a legendary Waziristani fighter, Mirza Ali Khan, Gul Bahadur is a senior and influential militant leader based in North Waziristan. Bahadur is known for hosting foreign militants, mainly al-Qaeda, as well as Maulana Jalaludin Haqqani, who runs a militia in Afghanistan. It is estimated that he has about 3,000 militants under his command, although there is no reliable information.

Mullah Nazir

A powerful militant commander based in North Waziristan, Mullah Nazir has cooperated with Pakistan's military in the past and led an operation against Uzbeks in the area. Nazir is supportive of the Pakistani military but has strong objections over the deployment of US-led coalition troops in Afghanistan. He has even said that he would be happy to take Osama bin Laden as a guest if he visits Nazir's area.

Maulana Faqir Mohammad

Based in Bajaur agency, Maulana Faqir Mohammad is a close associate of Baitullah Mehsud. A former leader of the banned Islamic group Tehrik-e Nifaze Shariat-e Mohammadi (TNSM) that is active in NWFP's Swat area, he is considered the manager of TTP's "outreach" operations in NWFP. He is a resident of Sewai village in Bajaur's Mamond area, a stronghold for the

Pakistani Taliban. Mohammad's forces resisted the Pakistani security forces in 2008. In early 2009, the military campaign has diminished his group's strength and disrupted his command structure and supply routes to other tribal regions, as well as Afghanistan's Kunar and Nuristan provinces.

Waliur Rahman (Raihan)

Leader of Jaish-e Islami, a group of militants hailing from the Bajaur village of Damadola that was attacked by Predator drones in 2006 and 2008. Due to these attacks, Damadola enjoys special status with the militants in FATA and especially in Bajaur agency.

Omar Khalid (or Abdul Wali)

A rebellious Taliban leader based in Mohmand agency. He challenged some of the directions of Baitullah Mehsud, but otherwise is known to be in his camp.

The WANA 5

After militant leader Nek Mohammad's killing in South Waziristan in 2004, a group of five people emerged in the area to enforce peace in the agency: Haji Omar, his brother Haji Sharif Khan, Javed Karmazkhel, Maulana Abdul Aziz, and Maulana Mohammad Abbas. The government subsequently made a peace deal with this shura.

Hakimullah Mehsud

Originally from South Waziristan, Hakimullah Mehsud is a young regional commander of the Pakistani Taliban who has set up bases in the Lower Kurram Valley and Khyber agency.

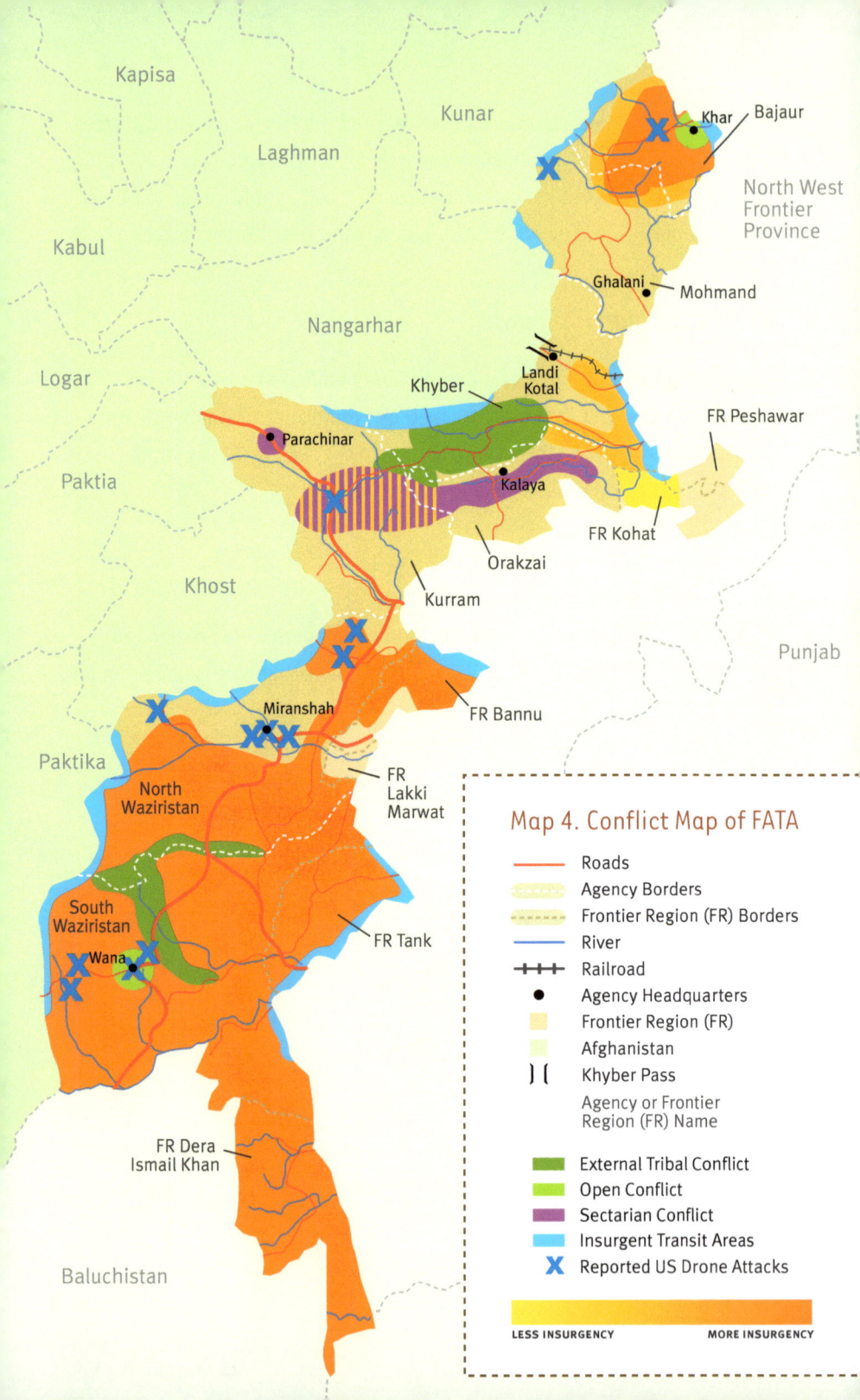

Map 4. Conflict Map of FATA

Places labeled on map: Kapisa, Laghman, Kunar, Kabul, Logar, Nangarhar, Paktia, Khost, Paktika, North West Frontier Province, Punjab, Baluchistan

Khar, Bajaur, Ghalani, Mohmand, Landi Kotal, Khyber, FR Peshawar, Parachinar, Kalaya, Orakzai, FR Kohat, Kurram, FR Bannu, Miranshah, FR Lakki Marwat, North Waziristan, FR Tank, South Waziristan, Wana, FR Dera Ismail Khan

Legend:
- Roads
- Agency Borders
- Frontier Region (FR) Borders
- River
- Railroad
- Agency Headquarters
- Frontier Region (FR)
- Afghanistan
- Khyber Pass
- Agency or Frontier Region (FR) Name
- External Tribal Conflict
- Open Conflict
- Sectarian Conflict
- Insurgent Transit Areas
- Reported US Drone Attacks

LESS INSURGENCY — MORE INSURGENCY

Kamran Mustafa Hijrat (Mohammad Yahya Hijrat)

Kamran Mustafa Hijrat is an important deputy in the Khyber agency. He was arrested by Pakistani security forces in Peshawar in December 2008 and is still being held.

Mangal Bagh Afridi

He leads a newer organization Lashkar-e Islam in the Khyber agency. He is anti-Taliban politically but his religious worldview is quite similar to the Taliban. Before becoming an *amir* (leader), he was a bus driver. He is a successor of Mufti Munir Shakir, a Deobandi cleric who set up a private radio network in the Khyber agency in 2004 after being thrown out of Kurram agency by tribal elders for inciting sectarianism. Shakir handed over his mobile radio station to Mangal Bagh later, according to local sources. He was pushed out by security forces from the agency in late 2008 during an operation, but his infrastructure and influence remain strong in his area. The weapons balance is shifting in FATA because insurgents have access to modern weapons and communications systems like satellite phones, but not tanks or airplanes. Insurgents are mobile, mostly relying on all-terrain, double-cab pickup trucks that al-Qaeda gave to them, according to some sources. The Taliban are also benefiting from an additional weapon of human resources: the demographic pressure in FATA from a young generation that is largely uneducated, unemployed, and ripe for recruitment for insurgency.

Maulana Sadiq Noor and Maulana Abdul Khaliq

Maulana Sadiq Noor and Maulana Abdul Khaliq are two other important militant leaders active in North Waziristan. Both are associated with Fazlur Rahman's Jamiat Ulema-e Islam-F (JUI-F; a Deobandi religious political party involved in mainstream electoral politics in Pakistan).

The Taliban's military field manual, Nizami Darsoona - Da Mujahideeno Da Aghdad La para, is written in Pashto, detailing jihad doctrine and the utility of different strategic options.

PHOTO BY IMTIAZ ALI

Chapter 8
Information and Influence

T he public generally depends on FM radio channels for news and information. Mosques and *hujras* are the places where they discuss news and information. The local Pashtun population prefers to listen to and believe the news contained in local broadcasts rather than broadcasts beamed from Western countries. They want local information in local dialects and community ownership.

The Taliban and their affiliates use radio in FATA to incite hatred and violence. According to a recent credible survey conducted in FATA by a local group, 35 percent of FATA's population listens to "unlicensed" and other international radio programming.

The Pakistani Taliban and its affiliates have been very active in producing propaganda CDs and DVDs. The contents include: last statements of suicide bombers; coverage of IED and suicide bombing attacks; and *jihadi* songs and lectures by popular militants on religious discourse and jihad concepts.

Various publications ("inspirational booklets," pamphlets, *fatwa* dissemination) are also available for those who can read. All these aspects constitute a well-designed and effective media and communications plan.

RADIO PROPAGANDA

Local militants use around 100 illegal FM radio stations. Some preach jihad against US and NATO forces in Afghanistan, others focus on only proselytizing. The illegal radio station phenomenon started in 2003 and now has become widespread practice. The number of illegal stations range between 75 and 125. Officials in the Pakistan Media Regulation Authority (PEMRA), the media watchdog, have counted 108 illegal FM radio stations in both FATA and NWFP. They collected these numbers from local police stations and FC units. According to their figures and assessment, these illegal radio stations are most effective and organized in Bajaur, Khyber, Orakzai, and Mohmand agencies.

Transmitters and Frequency

To set up an illegal radio station in a mosque or madrassa, the Taliban use a radiator-shaped transmitter, a basic amplifier, and a car battery. These components are inexpensive and easily available in NWFP and adjacent Afghan markets. According to local sources, an FM channel can cost from $500 to $1,000, depending on the transmitter's quality. PEMRA officials maintain that signals of most of the illegal FM channels work within 25-30 km. The more powerful FM transmitters have listeners within 50-60 km. These radio channels broadcast on an FM band that can be received by any conventionally available FM band receiver with a frequency range of 88-108

MHz. These channels have not been allocated frequencies by the Frequency Allocation Board (FAB). They simply begin broadcasting on a local FM frequency. In some areas, illegal FM radio stations operate at frequencies reserved for security agencies and police, jeopardizing these official communications.

Impact

Known as "FM mullahs," radical and extremist clerics use the airwaves to preach, prescribe appropriate behavior, incite villagers to engage in holy war, redefine the role of women in society, and intimidate populations by reciting the names of tribal leaders and security officials marked for death. At times, logistics such as the distribution of arms and mobilization of militants are also coordinated on air. The use of such illegal FM radio stations by two rival sectarian groups in the Khyber agency triggered bloody clashes between the groups.

The militant illegal radio stations primarily target the local communities in villages and towns of rural areas with the apparent aim of *Dars-e Qur'an* (translation and interpretation of the Koran) and promoting Islamic education and values. However, besides purely religious programs, discussions are primarily focused on political and regional issues. For instance, in Mohmand agency, clerics routinely give sermons and speeches supporting the Taliban, criticizing the Pakistani government, Hamid Karzai's government in Afghanistan, US operations against al-Qaeda fugitives in FATA, and what they frame as "the US occupation of Afghanistan." In many cases the radio hosts openly support resistance against US forces in Iraq and ask Muslims to liberate not only Iraq but other parts of the Muslim, world with special emphasis on the Arab-Israeli conflict. Even Mangal Bagh of the Khyber agency, who is not aligned with the

Pakistani or Afghan Taliban, openly supports the Taliban insurgency in Afghanistan and calls it a "Holy War" on his FM channel. Attacks on NATO storage facilities around Peshawar near the Khyber agency have also been encouraged by some FM stations in the Jamrud area of the Khyber agency.

The illegal radio stations are popular among women as contact with the outside world. According to local Pashto-language newspapers, all members of the family – men, women, and children – sit together and listen to the sermons on their transistors in many areas. Most of the broadcasts start in the evening when everyone has returned home from work. Broadcasts generally last one to two hours. They start soon after *maghrib* (sunset) prayer and continue until *esha* (night) prayer. Since most people in FATA are illiterate, radio is their primary means of mass communication.

Government Failure to Block FM Radios

Because these transmissions are being carried out by the religious centers (mosque and seminaries), PERMA officials argue that taking any action against them is a sensitive issue. Such actions will be deemed "un-Islamic," as religious education is also given through these programs. According to PEMRA officials, they had confiscated about 162 illegal FM radio stations in various parts of the NWFP between April 2007 and April 2009. The situation in FATA is more difficult because PEMRA cannot operate there directly. PERMA was created for four provinces of Pakistan and does not have jurisdiction in FATA. Some experts believe that the only solution to this growing menace is jamming the channels – not confiscating equipment. Since 2006, the government has made sporadic attempts to clamp down on illegal stations, often with raids or bombs. In a recent media report, FATA-based technicians claimed they were manufacturing broadcasting equipment now for less than Rs.15,000 (US $200) to face the challenge.

Recognizing the need for local programming to counter "FM Mullahs," the FATA Secretariat has given licenses to a handful of community radio stations. So far this strategy has had little impact because the national government restricts these licenses. Community stations are required to remain apolitical, emphasize entertainment programming, and borrow heavily from official Radio Pakistan. Stations are required to broadcast some programs in Urdu, but Pashto language programs from illegal stations are more popular within FATA. The government maintains that that they lack the technology to jam or block the illegal stations. They argue that their jamming (through their older equipment) could interfere with their own communication systems, which are important for intelligence information.

TALIBAN STRATEGY: PUBLICATIONS AND MEDIA "HANDLING"

In late 2008, the Taliban published the fourth edition of their military field manual, Nizami Darsoona – *Da Mujahideeno Da Aghdad La para* (Military Teachings for the Preparation of Mujahidin). The 158-page hard-copy book was published in February 2007 to attract and train new recruits. The fourth edition is written in Pashto, demonstrating that its purpose is primarily to assist Taliban fighters in Pakistan and Afghanistan. The detailed manual contains information and diagrams of various small-arms, ammunition, light and heavy weaponry, communication tools, and even chemical and explosives formulas, as well as a discussion about jihad doctrine.

According to Imtiaz Ali's article in CTC Sentinel (for reference see bibliography), the discussion of the jihad doctrine from the Taliban/al-Qaeda perspective challenges the traditional meaning of jihad. The book infers that armed struggle is the primary form of jihad. It strongly denounces the notion that only a Muslim ruler is entitled to wage a holy war, arguing that this is not necessary if a Muslim ruler is a puppet of "infidel forces." It declares jihad a prerequisite for the establishment of an Islamic state, clearly pointing out the goal of the Taliban movement. The book attempts to inspire readers to join groups such as al-Qaeda and the Taliban in order to fulfill their religious duty of jihad. It also supports the use of suicide bombing, while discussing how such martyrdom tactics inflict maximum damage on enemy forces. It attempts to answer critical religious questions, such as whether it is necessary to receive parental permission before participating in jihad, and offers religious justifications for suicide bombings. Similarly, it strongly supports the killing, and even the beheading, of spies who provide information to the enemy. In terms of jihad tactics, the field manual describes the relevance and utility of different options in specific circumstances – military, guerrilla, terrorist, spy, propaganda, economic, and nuclear. There is a long discussion of guerrilla and terrorist operations, declaring these to be most relevant for Afghanistan and global operations.

According to a March 2009 *Christian Science Monitor* report, residents of FATA are practically forced to choose between Radio Azadi, the Afghan Service of Radio Free Europe that broadcasts from Afghanistan, and the illegal transmissions of FM mullahs. The most popular illegal transmissions are: Mangal Bagh's *Lashkar-e Islam* radio service; Mufti Muneer Shakir's preaching service radio (on behalf of the Promotion of Virtue and Prevention of Vice group);

and lectures of "Tamachi (Pistol) Mullah," a cleric who urges his listeners to strike against Pakistanis who transport NATO supplies heading for Afghanistan. An alternative option is the "Voice of Khyber," a progressive station broadcasting in the Khyber agency's town of Jamrud that was launched in 2006 with official government support. As these channels (both illegal and legal) are highly dependent on call-ins from local residents, they are an excellent source for information for anyone who wants to monitor the groups associated with militancy and provoking violence.

In 1947, a jirga of the FATA maliks decided to join Pakistan, receiving assurances from the national government regarding their status. As such, many in FATA feel that the current deployment of the Pakistani army in FATA is a breach of these assurances.

PHOTO BY ANTHONY MAW

Appendices

FRONTIER REGIONS (FR)

There are six transitional areas wedged between FATA and NWFP that are called Frontier Regions (FR): FR Peshawar, FR Kohat, FR Bannu, FR Tank, FR Dera Ismail Khan, and FR Lakki Marwat. These FRs are administered by the provincial government through district coordination officers (DCO), previously known as deputy commissioners, of the respective NWFP district (for example, the DCO of Tank administers FR Tank). DCOs have similar roles as political agents.

Table 8. District Coordination Officers (FRs) – Contact Details

DISTRICT COORDINATION OFFICERS	CONTACT NO.
Sahibzada M. Anees, FR Peshawar	091-9212302
M. Javed Marwat, FR Bannu	0928-9270032
Syed Mohsin Shah, FR D. I. Khan	0966-9280116
Mr. Siraj Ahmad, FR Kohat	0922-9260032; 0922-513484
M. Anwar Khan Mehsud, FR Lakki Marwat	0969-538330; 0969-538331
Mr. Barkat Ullah, FR Tank	0963-510200

Source: Government of Pakistan Directory, 2009

Table 9. Population, Size and Tribal Affiliations of FRs

FR	POPULATION/AREA	TRIBES
FR Peshawar	66,816/ 261 sq. km	Afridis
FR Kohat	113,743/446 sq. km	Afridis
FR Bannu	242,44/745 sq. km	Ahmadzai Waziris; Uthmanzai Waziris; Bhittanis
FR Lakki Marwat	8,646/132 sq. km	Bhittanis
FR Tank	33,677/1221 sq. km	Bhittanis
FR Dera Ismail Khan	48,247/2008 sq. km	Shiranis, Usthrans

Source: Bureau of Statistics, Planning and Development Department, Government of NWFP

The six frontier regions are governed under the FCR and, for all practical purposes, are considered similar in status (legally and constitutionally) to the seven tribal agencies of FATA. DCOs recruit and provide benefits to their respective lungi holders and khassadars according to their service to the government and as per quota of each tribe living in the area. However, their economies and management are more closely linked to NWFP because their political administrators function as officials of NWFP.

FR Peshawar

FR Peshawar is bordered on the north by Ghari Chandan village of Peshawar district, on the south by Darra Adam Khel of FR Kohat, on the east by Jaroba, Cherat, Saleh Khana, and Spin Khak of Nowshera district, and on the west again by Peshawar district. Many families from tribes living in the surrounding areas live in the hilly terrain of FR Peshawar, most notably Bunerwal, Chagarzai, Chamlawal, and Khundu Khel sections of the Yousafzai; the Uthmankhel; the Gadun (also called Jadoon in a different part of NWFP); the Mohmand; and the Safi.

FR Kohat

FR Kohat is bordered on the north by FR Peshawar and Khyber agency, on the east by Nowshera district, on the south by Kohat district, and on the west by Orakzai agency. The Kohat Pass is similar to to the Khyber Pass as a historic highway of invasion. This area is also noto- rious for its arms manufacturing industry in Darra Adam Khel. Darra Adam Khel became a gun factory area in 1897, and British forces were guaranteed safe passage along the main route passing through the area in turn for looking the other way. A wide variety of firearms are produced in the town, from anti-aircraft guns to pen guns. Weapons are handmade by individual craftsmen using traditional manufac- turing techniques handed down from father to son. The quality of the guns is below average, but they are replicas of foreign made guns in shape and appearance. About 70 percent of the people in Darra Adam Khel are involved in this business. Though Punjab is the major export market for these weapons, NWFP and Afghanistan's border region also are important consumers.

The national government tried to encourage the arms manufacturers in Darra to take part in international defense weapons exhibitions held annually in major Pakistani cities in order to introduce the tribesmen to the international arms market and create business opportunities for them that are easily regulated and monitored. The move backfired, however, as most of the tradesmen started accusing the government of channeling the international orders to a selected few. According to government records, about 2,000-odd households are involved in exporting the weapons.

FR Bannu

Almost entirely rural, this area is bordered by Karak district to the north, by Bannu district to the east and south, by FR Lakki Marwat to the south, and by North Waziristan agency to the west. About one third of the total area is arable, but there is no major concentration of population since people live in small hamlets called *kotkas*. Due to intense heat in the summer, the majority of the population migrates to the hills of Shawal and Birmal in North and South Waziristan, which strongly connects them with the politics and influences of those tribal agencies.

FR Lakki Marwat

Bifurcated from FR Bannu in 1996, FR Lakki Marwat is hilly and rural. The culture of the area is greatly influenced by North Waziristan, connecting it with three important districts in NWFP: Karak, Bannu, and Lakki Marwat. The Taliban made inroads into the NWFP through this route in recent years.

FR Tank

This area is mainly inhabited by Bhittanis – a tribe that differs in many ways from other tribes of FATA and the Frontier Regions. Bhittanis are organized on tribal lines, but the leadership role in the tribe is more broadly distributed because there is no elite group or chief of the tribe. The proverbial wit of the countryside reflects their character: "The drum was beating in the plains and the Bhittanis were dancing on the hills," "A hundred Bhittanis eat a hundred sheep," meaning that each Bhittanis considers himself to be equal to the other and they do not accept someone as their chief. They also discarded the dress of their neighbors of the Waziristan highlands for the dress of the plains, and their local dialect is different from other Pashto dialects of the neighboring areas. Importantly, they are considered the hereditary enemies of the Mehsuds for helping the British fight them.

FR D.I. Khan

Also known as Argha Shirani Area, it is known for *Takht-e Sulaiman* – believed to be "Soloman's throne," a shrine on the mountain of the Sulaiman range, also known as the Kaisargarh or Kasi Ghar. According to local tradition, Solomon halted on a ledge some distance below the crest of the mountain to take a last look over India, when he was carrying off an Indian bride to Jerusalem. The shrine marks the spot.

FATA PERSPECTIVES

To understand the dynamics in FATA in more details, it is critical to look at the perspectives of the people of FATA and their inspirations, complaints, and concerns. It is equally important to look at the strategies being adopted by Taliban. Only then can one delve into the sphere of potential drivers of change.

Ordinary people of FATA believe that:

- Their blood and tribal relations with their brethren in Afghanistan are critical to their identity and survival, and they must support Afghans in pushing the foreigners out.

- The Durand Line is no more than a line in the sand. They do not recognize it.

- They cherish the fact that they provided a platform for the Pakistani army and its intelligence services to train, arm, and finance the anti-Soviet insurgency in Afghanistan during the 1980s.

- They had accepted Arabs and Uzbeks and Uigher "guests" who had come to help their cause and then settled, learning their language, marrying their women, and settling down in the area. They consider it against pashtunwali code to now hand them over to anyone or ask them to leave the area.

- The Pakistani army's operations in FATA led to a very high level of collateral damage. These military strikes are seen as "America's war" that the Pakistani army is waging, killing its own people. Local people in FATA think that the US wants to occupy the strategic areas of Pashtuns and use this as base for exploiting the resources of the whole region in the name of the war on terror. Generally, the people of FATA are extremely critical of the US/NATO presence in Afghanistan. The reason why many FATA militants are conducting suicide attacks in Islamabad and other urban areas of Pakistan is that they consider Pakistani leadership to be playing into the hands of Americans.

- The very presence of the army in FATA is seen as a violation of the arrangement that FATA maliks had finalized with the government of Pakistan in 1947.

Pakistan's government (army, ISI, civilian bureaucracy) believes that:

- Pakistan is unfairly blamed for everything that has gone wrong in Afghanistan. Lack of investment in developing infrastructure of Afghanistan, failure to eradicate opium production, and poor governance has reignited Taliban fervor and insurgency.

- Pakistan has been pushed to fight the extremists against public opinion in the country, whereas the path of negotiations and "peace deals" would have led to better results.

- Indian influence and the preference of Tajik and Uzbek elements in the power structure of Afghanistan are seen as threats to Pakistan's interests in Afghanistan (which are linked to dominance of Pashtuns in Afghanistan). Pakistan suspects that both India and Afghanistan are supporting Baluch insurgents inside Pakistan.

- Pakistan also feels that the concentration of Indian consulates in the eastern part of Afghanistan is a threat to its national stability, which in turn could minimize Pakistan's military focus on Kashmir – the bone of contention between the two countries.

- Many smugglers, drug dealers, and criminals have also moved to FATA, and the crisis is not solely due to religious extremists or the Taliban. (The Taliban movement has been joined by several other criminal gangs like smugglers, drug dealers, etc.)

- There is skepticism about the long-term US agenda in the region. This is partly influenced by Pakistan's strategic relations with China, as well as by the belief that the civilian nuclear arrangement between the US and India has made the two countries very close.

FURTHER READING AND SOURCES

Useful Links

- FATA Development Authority: *http://fatada.gov.pk/*
- FATA official website: *www.fata.gov.pk*
- CSIS Report: *www.csis.org/media/csis/pubs/ 080917_afghanthreat.pdf*
- Khyber agency: *www.khyber.gov.pk*
- SWDO: *www.swdo.org*
- Parachinar: *http://parachinar616.blogspot.com/*
- IPRI Paper: *http://ipripak.org/papers/federally.shtml*
- Cost of Conflict in FATA: *www.fata.gov.pk/downloads/ costconflict.pdf*
- FATA Education Data: *www.fata.edu.pk/Final%20FATA2007-08%20 Publication.pdf*
- Pakistan's Tribal Areas, Council on Foreign Relations: *www.cfr.org/publication/11973/*
- NWFP Bureau of Statistics: *http://nwfp.gov.pk/BOS/myepfata07.htm*
- Understanding FATA: *www.understandingfata.org*
- Insight into Pakistan's Conflict: Q&A with Khalid Aziz: *http://changinguppakistan.wordpress.com/2009/04/27/ insight-into-pakistans-conflict-qa-with-khalid-aziz/*
- Asian Development Bank Report (2006): *www.adb.org/documents/rrps/pak/33268-PAK-RRP.pdf*
- Frontier Corps: *www.khyber.org/pashtohistory/frontiercorps/ frontiercorps.shtml*

- FATA timeline: *www.satp.org/satporgtp/countries/pakistan/*
  Waziristan/timeline/index.html

Local NGOs

- Small and Medium Enterprises Development Authority (SMEDA):
  www.smeda.org.pk/

- Pakistan Stone Development Company (PASDEC):
  www.pasdec.org/

- National Centre of Excellence in Geology, University of Peshawar
  (NECG): *http://nceg.upesh.edu.pk/*

- Tribal Chamber of Commerce and Industry (TACCI)

International NGOs

- DAI: *www.dai.com*

- IUCN: the International Union for Conservation of Nature:
  www.iucn.org

- USAID: United States Agency for International Development:
  www.usaid.gov/

- DFID: United Kingdom Department for International Development:
  www.dfid.gov.uk/

- IMC: International Medical Corps: *http://imcworldwide.org/*

Reports on FATA

- Hassan Abbas, "Policy Options for President Obama's Policy
  Options in Pakistan's FATA," ISPU, Institute for Social Policy
  and Understanding January 2009.

- Shuja Nawaz, "FATA: A Most Dangerous Place,"
  Center for Strategic and International Studies, January 2009.

- Daniel Markey, "Securing Pakistan's Tribal Belt,"
  Council on Foreign Relations, August 2008.

- Joshua T. White, "Pakistan's Islamist Frontier,"
  Center on Faith & International Affairs, 2008.

- FATA Sustainable Development Plan 2006-2015,
  Government of Pakistan.

Books and Articles

- Abbas, Hassan, "A Profile of Tehrik-i-Taliban Pakistan," *CTC Sentinel*,
  volume 1, issue 2, pages 1-4, January 2008.

- Abbas, Hassan (ed.). "Pakistan's Troubled Frontier,"
  Jamestown Foundation, 2009.

- Ali, Imtiaz, "Preparing the Mujahidin: The Taliban's Military
  Field Manual," *CTC Sentinel*, Volume 1, Issue 10, pages 5-7,
  September 2008.

- Barfield, Thomas. "The Durand Line: History, Consequence and
  Future," The American Institute of Afghan Studies, *Conference
  Report*, 2007.

- Beattie, Hugh. *Imperial Frontier: Tribe and State in Waziristan*.
  Richmond: Curzon Press, 2002.

- Fair, C. Christine. *The Madrassah Challenge: Militancy and Religious
  Education in Pakistan*. Washington D.C.: United States Institute of
  Peace Press, 2008.

- *International Crisis Group*. "Pakistan's Tribal Areas: Appeasing the
  Militants." Asia Report 125, 11 (December 2006).

- Johnson, Thomas, and M. Chris Mason. "No Sign until the Burst of Fire: Understanding the Pakistan-Afghanistan Frontier." *International Security*, Vol. 34, No. 2 (Spring 2008): 41-77.

- Kaplan, Robert. *Soldiers of God*. New York: Vintage Departures, 2001.

- Khan, Mukhtar A., "The FM Mullahs and Taliban's Propaganda War in Pakistan," *The Jamestown Foundation*, Terrorism Monitor; Volume 7, issue 14; May 26, 2009.

- Rashid, Ahmed. *Descent Into Chaos*. London: Viking, 2008.

- Roy, Olivier. "Afghanistan: Back to Tribalism or on to Lebanon?" *Third World Quarterly*, 11 No. 4 (October 1989): 70-82.

- US Congress. House Committee on House Foreign Affairs. Subcommittee on the Middle East and South Asia. *US-Pakistan Relations: Assassination, Instability, and the Future of US Policy*. January 16, 2008.

- United States Government Accountability Office. "Combating Terrorism: The United States Lacks Comprehensive Plan to Destroy the Terrorist Threat and Close the Safe Haven in Pakistan's Federally Administered Tribal Areas." April 2008.

- Yusuf, Huma, "Pakistan's Airwaves: On Militant Turf, Radio Khyber Offers a Softer Voice", *Christian Science Monitor*, March 13, 2009.

www.ingramcontent.com/pod-product-compliance
Lightning Source LLC
Chambersburg PA
CBHW040127270326
41927CB00001B/17